MANAGING PEOPLE

Managing People

JANE and CHRIS CHURCHOUSE

A Gower Management Workbook

Published by
Gower Publishing Limited
Gower House
Croft Road
Aldershot
Hampshire GU1 3HR
England

Gower
Old Post Road
Brookfield
Vermont 05036
USA

British Library Cataloguing in Publication Data

Churchouse, Jane
    Managing people. – (A Gower management workbook)
    1. Personnel management
    I. Title II. Churchouse, Chris
    658.3

ISBN 0 566 08015 X

Typeset by Mind*Shift* Ltd and printed in Great Britain by MPG Books, Bodmin.

Contents

PART III 'Managing would be easy if it were not for the people'
How to manage performance and discipline problems

Get to know how the legal system acts

Get to know your organization's procedures

Checklist for a disciplinary procedure

Preface

The days are gone when management texts had to be long and dull. Nowadays it is recognized that most managers are very busy and are interested in practical books that will actually help them to manage better. We have written this Workbook with the busy practical manager very much in mind. You will not find long expositions of some theory, backed up by impenetrable statistics, graphs or tables. Instead, you will find a range of workaday solutions to the sorts of problem that most managers face at some time in their careers.

You will see that the book is split into various sections – known as 'Parts' – and subsections or 'Units'. Each Part begins with a brief explanation of what you can expect to find in it and a self-assessment test. If you are happy that you can answer all the questions in the test you do not need to read through the whole of the Part – simply scan the 'Fast Track' sections of each Unit as a refresher and then move on. If, however, you would like to increase your knowledge and understanding in any of the area covered by the questions, the whole of the 'Skillbuilder' section in each Unit is for you.

At the end of the Workbook you will find some final activities (which you might like to use towards an NVQ or similar qualification) together with some further reading and useful addresses in case you want to follow a particular topic through.

Thank you for choosing to read *Managing People*. Good luck! We hope you enjoy it.

Jane and Chris Churchouse

Acknowledgements

Acknowledgements are due to all our friends and learners who, over the years, have never failed to shed new light on old problems. We may have learned more from them than they have from us!

About the Authors

Jane Churchouse

Jane holds an Honours Degree, a Master's Degree in Business Administration (MBA), various teaching and training qualifications, NVQs in Management and in Training and certificates in psychometric testing. She is a Fellow of the Institute of Personnel and Development – for which she sits on the National Membership and Education Committee – and has been an External Verifier for an NVQ Awarding Body.

Jane's background is in personnel, training and line management with organizations such as British Airports Authority, Racal Telecom and the Department of Employment. She is now a Director of Mind*Shift* Ltd. where she specializes in providing consultancy and training in management and the implementation and delivery of NVQs.

Chris Churchouse

Chris holds a Degree in Mathematics and Technology and a Master's Degree in Business Administration (MBA). He is a member of the British Computer Society and the Institute of Management – for which he has been local Branch Chairman. He has been active in both organizations at national level, in various committees and working parties.

His working career has encompassed spells in both the private and public sectors with organizations such as Dexion, Westland Helicopters and the Ministry of Defence, concentrating initially on engineering and information technology and, latterly, on the people side of project management. He is a qualified PRINCE project management practitioner and a Chartered IS Engineer. Chris is also a Director of Mind*Shift* Ltd, having laid the foundation for the organization in October 1986.

'I've just trained Sally and she's left to get a better job...!'

How to manage staff recruitment and selection

Introduction

By the end of **Part I** you will be able to:

- respond in a structured way to someone's resignation
- use recruitment techniques that are appropriate to the job
- take a rigorous and fair approach to staff selection
- describe how to conduct a competent selection interview.

If you are confident that you can already answer 'Yes' to most or all of the following questions you might like simply to refresh your memory by scanning the Fast Track pages in each Unit and then move on to Part II.

Self-assessment Checklist: Part I	
I am confident that I can:	**Yes ☑ No ☒**
explain how job design can affect motivation at work	
outline the differences between a job description and a person specification	
describe what a 'critical incident' interview is and how I could use it	
outline the relevant provisions of at least six UK employment laws	
illustrate the different answers I can expect to questions beginning 'Did you ...?' and 'How did you ...?'	
explain the use of at least four different selection tools	
describe the 'equal partner' approach to selection	

UNIT 1 What to Do When Someone Leaves

In this Unit, we will be covering the three actions you need to take to respond to someone's resignation in a structured way – that is:

- **find out why they're leaving**
- **use the opportunity to review the work**
- **make your decision.**

Understanding these three actions will help you:

- decide whether or not to encourage them to stay
- review the way your department currently operates and maximize on the opportunity for change.

What to Do When Someone Leaves

You may be wondering why we have started this book on managing people in such a seemingly negative way. The reason is simple: this is the action most likely to trigger a whole series of events that encompass the gamut of people management.

In this Fast Track section, we show you what to do if you are currently faced with a resignation. On the following page is a concept diagram, showing the steps that you need to go through to make a good decision about what is happening now. We expand the concept diagram over the following pages and, by the end of the Fast Track section, you should know precisely what you need to do.

Once you have dealt with your immediate needs, you can, if you wish, take some time to work through the Skillbuilder section. This will help you to build up your knowledge and skills so that, in the future, you will be able to handle resignations more expertly.

We have used this approach throughout the Workbook: Fast Track to deal with an immediate situation, followed by a Skillbuilder to help you develop your abilities.

CONCEPT DIAGRAM: RESIGNATIONS

Step 1: Find out why they are leaving

Ask
them why they
want to leave

Consider
whether you want
them to stay

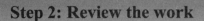

Step 2: Review the work

Examine
work objectives
of section or
department

Review
terms and conditions

Review
the nature of the job

Assess
the workload

Review
the person's abilities

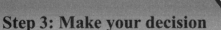

Step 3: Make your decision

	You want them to stay	You do not want them to stay
There is no job	Look at other jobs for them	Accept their resignation
The job has changed	Look at changing their skills, terms and so forth to match	Recruit someone into the new job
The job is the same	Negotiate to keep them	Recruit a replacement

STEP 1: FIND OUT WHY THEY ARE LEAVING

People leave jobs for a variety of reasons and may not tell you the true one, even if you ask them. Nevertheless, finding out why someone wants to leave may help you persuade them to stay, or may help you make changes in the job or the workplace to improve your staff retention in the future. You may find out how your business could become more attractive to staff, or ways in which it could be more efficient, so your first step must be to ask.

Your discussion should be short, and you should not make any promises or statements that you might regret later. Listen to the reply and ask clarifying questions if you need to. If they tell you that they want to leave because they have been offered a better job elsewhere, you should ask them what made them start looking elsewhere. After all, if they were perfectly happy with the job, the rewards, their career prospects and so on, they would not have been looking for a change.

You may also consider looking at trends. Have many people left this department, or even this job, recently? What reasons have they given?

In this way, you have left the door open for whatever action you eventually decide is appropriate. The member of staff knows that you have understood their position and that you will be making enquiries about them, their job and workloads generally. They also know that the discussion they have just had with you is not the only one they will have.

Finally, you need to make an early decision after your meeting, and for your own information only, about whether you would like this person to stay. You may need to look at their personnel record or to talk discreetly to other managers or supervisors in order to do this.

It is worth doing this even if their decision is based on entirely personal reasons such as moving away. Even the most definite reasons can sometimes be changed.

You now have the resignation situation under control and can proceed to the next step.

STEP 2: USE THE OPPORTUNITY TO REVIEW THE WORKLOAD

There are several actions that you now need to take, although you will not always do them in the same order. First, consider the job and the wider workload and staffing issues that you are facing, rather than concentrate solely on the person resigning. Here are some areas to look at.

Look at the work objectives of the section or department concerned. Do you really need the same type of job? If you do, you may wish to reassess the workload to see whether it could be distributed among existing staff, in which case you will need to take their views into account.

Find out if there are any other vacancies in your department, or elsewhere.

Look at the terms and conditions. Is it essential that someone comes in to do the work, or could they be home-based? Could you be flexible about the hours, enabling people with home commitments to do the job?

Look into the nature of the job. Is it particularly boring, or does it need a lot of concentration? If so, filling it with two part-timers may be a better option than taking on someone full-time. How does it fit in with the work of other members of the team? Would it be possible to make it more autonomous so that the person doing it feels that they are making a worthwhile contribution?

Now it is time to bring in information about the person. If you have discovered some new opportunity that might persuade this person to stay, you should consider what training or other developmental activities they would need. You should check on any regulations (legal or organizational) about what to do when someone leaves. Check what you are permitted to negotiate and how to go about either retaining them or letting them go.

Check the consequences of any potential changes to working conditions or salary and so forth. You need to ensure that you are not setting yourself up for disgruntled workers who feel that this person has received special treatment – especially if they perceive this as discrimination.

STEP 3: MAKE YOUR DECISION

Your decision will be based on the objective investigation which you have carried out around the job and the workload, plus your inevitably subjective opinions about the desirability of retaining this person.

The table from page 8 is repeated here and shows what action you need to take in each combination of circumstances.

We cover recruitment in Unit 2

	You want them to stay	**You do not want them to stay**
There is no job	Look at other jobs for them	Accept their resignation
The job has changed	Look at changing their skills, terms and so forth to match	Recruit someone into the new job
The job is the same	Negotiate to keep them	Recruit a replacement

Cross out any unacceptable outcomes. Rank the rest in terms of your preferences. Check that you have enough information about these options. Remember that this is your decision. The person concerned will also need to have an input into the final agreed outcome.

You therefore need to conduct a more in-depth interview. You now have all the information you require and you know what options are available to you and which are not. You also know your own preferred outcome and any possible fallback outcomes as well as the procedures you should follow and the extent of your bargaining power.

If your decision is to encourage them to stay, you will need to tell them what you have done and what options are open. Negotiate within the bounds that you have decided on or agreed with your own manager. Be open about offers of retraining or changing work conditions. Check that any agreed outcome will resolve the causes of their discontent. If you cannot come to an agreement, follow the corresponding action on the right side of the table. Otherwise, accept the person back into the organization and **do what you promised to do**.

If your decision is to accept their resignation, your job is to make their departure as easy for them and for you as you can. Thank them for the work they have done. Confirm their final day and any holiday entitlement they are taking. Arrange for the handover of any corporate property they may have. If they are in a job which allows them access to information, resources or clients such that their continued access could cause a problem, you may prefer to waive their notice period and ask them to leave immediately. Alternatively, you might require them to serve their notice period at home, without providing access to the sensitive information or contacts – something often referred to as 'gardening leave'.

Otherwise, allow them to return to their job and ask them to prepare a 'handover plan' so that the department can continue to operate when they have gone.

YOU MAY NOW CONTINUE WITH THE NEXT UNIT ON PAGE 23
OR MOVE TO THE SKILLBUILDER SECTION THAT FOLLOWS

What to Do When Someone Leaves

Managers often regard someone's resignation either as a personal insult or as demonstrating a heinous lack of loyalty on the part of the person they have striven so hard to manage well.

Although it can be hurtful when someone you have developed and taken an interest in suddenly hands in their notice, as a good manager you will want to look at the situation constructively and make the best of a bad job. So, you need to determine what has led to the resignation. It could be:

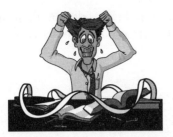

A genuine complaint about the job or the organization, which you need to tackle

Something to do with matters outside the workplace over which you have no control

A compliment that someone you have developed is so attractive to another organization

Part of life's ups and downs! A combination of effects

It is also an opportunity to review and improve the way the work is done, or the department is organized.

You must also be aware that, just because someone resigns, it does not mean you must try to make them stay – sometimes it is better to let them go. Your decision must therefore be based on a broad understanding of all the factors. The three-point approach which we have taken in the preceding Fast Track section allows you to do this in a constructive manner.

STEP 1: FIND OUT WHY THEY ARE LEAVING

People do not always tell you the real reason for leaving –
especially if they feel that to do so would compromise their
chances of getting a good reference, or might involve them in an
uncomfortable discussion from which they gain nothing.
Nevertheless, their reason(s) for leaving may help to guide you
through what to do next. The Fast Track section guides you
through what to do for a particular case. In this Skillbuilder
section, we deal with more general issues.

 **Activity**

Which of these factors do you think would make someone
want to resign? Rank them in order of likelihood.

Low salary	
Poor working conditions	
Lack of leadership from their manager	
Short holiday entitlement	
Lack of career prospects	
The nature of the work	
Poor relationship with colleagues	
Lack of personal development opportunities	

Research into the factors that motivate and demotivate people has
been conducted by Frederick Herzberg. He found that some
things made a difference when they were increased, while others
made a difference only by their absence (or insufficiency).
Strangely, he found that people were not motivated by extra pay
– they simply became less motivated if it was insufficient. (He
called these 'hygiene factors'.) People are often motivated by the
simplest things, such as their control over their working
conditions. Someone may actually resign because they don't like
windows that don't open! They just won't tell you that, because
they think it sounds silly. So they tell you it's because they 'want
a career change' or they 'want to work nearer to home'. You make
the wrong changes (or none at all) and the problem stands
uncorrected.

So, how might you discover the real causes of their resignation?
On the next page there is a questionnaire that you might use
periodically. Make sure it is returned anonymously and, even if
you do know who said something, do not confront them about it.

Job Satisfaction Questionnaire

This questionnaire is being used to find out how the organization can improve its working conditions and practices. Your help by completing it will assist us in making changes where we need to, although we cannot promise to attend immediately to every suggestion. Please return it to:

Do you consider your career prospects within the company to be good, poor, somewhere in between or of no importance to you?	Good Poor L_____I_____J Not important ☐
How much do you enjoy the tasks you have to do in your job?	A lot Not! L_____I_____J
Are the company's expectations of your personal development too high, too low, somewhere between, or do you not know?	Too high Too low L_____I_____J Don't know ☐
Would you like to have more control over what you do, more direction from your manager, or something in between?	Control Direction L_____I_____J
Are company procedures too rigid, too loose, or somewhere in between?	Rigid Loose L_____I_____J
Please list up to five things that have particularly pleased you about your job here over the past year.	1. 2. 3. 4. 5.
Please list up to five things that have particularly displeased you about your job here over the past year.	1. 2. 3. 4. 5.

If you have any suggestions for improvements to your work or your working conditions, please make a note of them here:

This questionnaire is only an example. When you design your own questionnaire, make sure that the layout allows adequate space for the responses. Also, ensure that the words you use will be familiar to your workforce – not everyone knows what 'autonomy' means and some may even struggle with the word 'perceive'.

STEP 2: USE THE OPPORTUNITY TO REVIEW THE WORKLOAD

This may be a good time to evaluate the work in your department. The nature of work does change over time and, all too soon, the jobs do not align with the people doing them. Work through the questions in the following checklist.

Area	Questions	Notes
Examine the work objectives of your department	Do you need to fill the same types of job? Do the current jobs match the job descriptions?	*You may be surprised at how jobs change over time. Now is a good time to take a fresh look at what you need.*
Reassess the workload	Must all jobs be full-time? Could you use part-timers? Could work be distributed better between existing members of staff? Would this represent a problem or an opportunity to them?	*Not everyone is looking for full-time employment. Redistributing the workload may be welcomed by staff – or not! How you handle any changes may be more important than the changes themselves.*
Look at the terms and conditions	Must the work be office or factory based? Could it be done by someone home-based? Could you be flexible about the hours, enabling people with home commitments to do the job?	*Keep an open mind. You may find a really good solution. Could you employ a disabled person or a student?*
Look at the nature of the job	Is any task particularly boring? Does it require a great deal of concentration? Does it require interaction with others in a team? How autonomous could it be?	*If a task is boring or requires much concentration, filling it with two part-timers may be a better option than taking on someone full-time. Some people like active jobs, some like to 'plod', some like to talk, some want to feel their work is valued by colleagues. What sort of person should do each task?*

You can add anything else to the checklist that you think is appropriate. The real key is to keep an open mind. Don't do something because you have always done it that way. Do it because it is the best way forward. Often the two will be the same, but not always.

As a further aid in determining the type of work that your department does, you may like to work through the next activity. It is based on our Star Tip for the section, which you should read as an introduction.

 Star Tip

During the 1980s, Hackman and Oldham suggested that the most motivating jobs contain certain features which have implications for job design. The features are:

* **Skill variety:** the extent to which the work requires a range of skills
* **Task identity:** the extent to which the work provides a whole, identifiable outcome
* **Task significance:** the extent to which the work has an impact on others (or, possibly, on oneself – as with research work)
* **Autonomy:** the extent of choice and discretion
* **Feedback from the job:** the extent to which the work itself provides feedback on how well it is being performed

Now use the questionnaire on the following page – you may like to copy it several times to cover each of the jobs in your department.

Alternatively, make photocopies of the questionnaire and ask the job-holders to fill them in. After all, they are the ones most likely to know about the nature of their tasks. You might like to compare your perceptions with theirs, to see how well you know your own department.

You will need to be aware of the different ways in which people can interpret the questions, however. If you ask job-holders to complete this questionnaire you may need to rephrase some questions and delete others. You will also need to provide some sort of introduction, to say what you are doing and to give guidance on how to complete the form. After all, the idea is to find out what issues need to be changed so that people want to stay – not to incite unrest so that they leave!

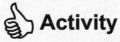 **Activity**

Job Design Questionnaire

Where scales are given, make a mark on each to show where on the range your answer lies.

Job Title:	
Skill variety: how varied are the skills needed?	Not at all Considerably
Task identity: how aware is the job-holder of how their work contributes to that of the business?	Not at all Highly aware
Task significance: how much does the job matter to the job-holder, or to others?	Not at all Has a high significance
Autonomy: how much choice and discretion does the job-holder have?	None Lots
Feedback from the job: how much does *the work itself* provide feedback to the job-holder on performance?	Does not provide feedback Provides strong feedback
Could the job be performed away from the workplace – at home, for example?	
Could the job be split between two people?	
How much does the workload fluctuate, and on what basis? What is the cycle?	
How closely does the job align with the current job description. Give examples of differences.	

STEP 3: MAKE YOUR DECISION

On page 8 of the Fast Track section, we presented you with a table to help your decision-making. You may like to use the same thinking process to review your department's current situation and decide what you would do for each person now working for you. You might be able to identify some potential job changes that could, if implemented now, prevent a resignation in the future. You might identify a person who is, for some reason, underperforming or in need of training or motivation. Training is often seen as expensive – but it is often cheaper than recruiting and inducting a new employee.

Here is the same table, reworded to make it more generally applicable to a department. Work through it now, or over a period of time.

	You want to keep all your staff	There are some who you would be prepared to let go
Some jobs have disappeared	Look at other jobs for them	Perhaps it's time to look at redundancy
Some jobs have changed	Review training needs, and terms – see Part II for more details	Monitor the situation. You may be into redundancy and recruitment
No changes at this time	Find ways to continue motivating them – see Part II for details	Live with it, or look at job performance – see Part III for more details

The final activity in this section is a reflective one. It calls upon your past experiences of resignations – your own and those of others – to help you understand the mental processes that a member of staff uses when they are facing resignation. By understanding these processes better, you should be able to appreciate why someone is leaving and fully understand their reasoning. This may improve your chances of success in changing their mind, or it may help you identify the real changes that are needed in the workplace.

 **Activity**

Review recent resignations. What reasons were given? How did you go about dealing with them? How happy have you been with their replacements?

Person who left	Their given reason(s)	Satisfaction with replacement

Review your own past resignations. What were your reasons – and what did you tell your employer? How happy have you been with the job you took instead? How similar or different was that new job to the one you resigned from, and in what ways?

Where from	Real reason	Reason you gave	How new job measured up

SKILLBUILDER

 **Case Study**

People will sometimes resign for no better reason than they feel undervalued and unrecognized. They can be particularly vulnerable when they have been passed over for promotion.

A friend of mine, Dee, came second on her promotion panel and was asked to report to the person who came first. Rather than talk through her reactions and agree the way in which she liked to work, Dee's new manager simply avoided her. Similarly, Dee's old manager made no efforts to facilitate the handover and make Dee feel that her opinions were valued.

Within two months Dee had resigned. She gave her reason as 'a better paid job elsewhere' and her manager accepted that there was nothing to be done about such a reason. Dee left the organization with very bitter feelings, and without her expertise the department really struggled to survive.

The next time that someone is promoted to a managerial position in Dee's old company, there is every likelihood that the situation will be repeated and the lesson will still not have been learned.

SKILLBUILDER

Dee was apparently in a position to be able to resign; other disgruntled members of staff may not be so well placed. This leads to a different situation to the one we have been looking at as, if you're not careful, people like this can become disruptive influences on everyone around them. We'll be looking at this kind of situation again – and what you can do about it – in Part III of the Workbook.

UNIT 2 — Three Steps to Effective Recruitment

In this Unit, we will be covering the three actions you need to take to find suitable candidates to fill your vacancies, which are to:

- **analyse your requirements**
- **write a job description and person specification**
- **choose appropriate recruitment media.**

Understanding these three actions will help you:

- decide what you are looking for in the ideal candidate – and what you can happily settle for if you don't find them
- make the sort of people you are looking for aware of your vacancy – and encourage them to apply for it.

Three Steps to Effective Recruitment

In Unit 1 you will already have seen how important it is to analyse your requirements before you take further action. We will continue the theme of offering you some advice in Fast Track on what you can do if you have an immediate recruitment need, and then follow this up in the Skillbuilder section with further work that will help you in the future.

However you arrived at your current requirement to recruit, you will first need to analyse your requirements, and this is where we start the section.

STEP 1: ANALYSE YOUR REQUIREMENTS

Taking people on is an expensive business and we need to give ourselves a fighting chance of doing a good job by arranging job tasks that are meaningful and that can reasonably be performed by a single individual.

How will you decide on your present requirements? As you have an immediate need, you probably do not have time to look deeply into your recruitment procedures or set this specific job into a wider context. This means concentrating on what you now need, and tackling the bigger issues later. Which of the following actions can you reasonably take right now?

1

Think through the most important aspects of the work – the 'critical success factors' – and what skills are needed to ensure success.

2

You can ask those people who will be influenced most by the new job-holder. What do they expect the person to do?

3

If you are replacing someone who has left (or been promoted or transferred), you may already have information about the job – in a job description, preferably.

We cover job descriptions in the next Step.

4

If the job-holder has not yet left, you can ask them about their job – what do they do, how do they do it, which elements are most important, who do they interact with, and so forth.

5

If the job is one of many similar ones, you may also like to consider a technique called 'critical incident interviewing'. This is where you interview several people who are really good at the job and several others who (with hindsight) you wish you had never employed. You ask them to describe incidents that they consider they have handled very well, or that they would like to have handled better, and see whether there are any patterns that separate the good performers from the weaker ones. These are the factors to concentrate on when selecting replacement staff. We describe critical incident technique more in the Skillbuilder section.

You may or may not be surprised to know that it is often the 'softer' skills that determine whether a person will be good at a job – whether they will fit in with a team and with the organization. Job-specific skills can be acquired by training, whereas attitudes to quality, team support, honesty, loyalty and so on are often very much harder to change. It is therefore better to recruit someone with the right attitudes and train them in the job-specific skills than to take on a technical wizard who will be unable to work in your organizational situation.

STEP 2: WRITE A JOB DESCRIPTION AND PERSON SPECIFICATION

A job description describes what the job-holder has to do, who they report to, what staff they have and what other responsibilities and authority they have.

A person specification describes the sort of person who would be suitable to take on in the job role. It may include physical attributes, knowledge, attitudes and so forth.

You will probably find that the information which you have collected when analysing your requirements covers aspects of both the job itself and the person best suited to do it, and you now need to separate them out. If you leave them mixed together, you will risk recruiting the wrong sort of person into an ill-defined role and end up very soon rereading Unit 1 – what to do when someone leaves.

If there is already a job description, make sure it is updated according to your analysis. If there is no job description, you should write one. If your organization has a standard format, use that. If not, here is a format that you can use.

 Example

Job title: Post Room Supervisor

Context: The job-holder reports to the Administration Manager and is responsible for three post room staff.

Job summary: To ensure that the work of the post room staff is performed in accordance with the agreed performance standards. Specifically, to manage the post room staff, to allocate work, to check that work is performed to standard and to maintain discipline within the post room.

Job content: To allocate work to post room staff and coordinate leave and breaks to ensure an adequate coverage of service.
To ensure that outgoing post is collected at agreed times from collection points.
To ensure that incoming post is distributed to individuals without delay, and that any necessary signatures (such as for registered post) are obtained and recorded.
To ensure that equipment is maintained, including franking equipment licences.
To ensure that post room staff are adequately trained in the skills of their jobs, and in the Health and Safety requirements that apply to them.

Working conditions: Monday – Friday 8am to 4:30pm, with one hour for lunch. Lunches to be staggered within the post room. Salary to be at Band 3 level.

Performance standards: All incoming post must be distributed within two hours of receipt. Signatures must be obtained and recorded for registered post and other similar post. Outgoing post placed for collection before 3pm must be sent that day.

Now that you have written the job description, you need to determine what personal attributes will be required by someone who is to perform that job successfully.

A useful way of thinking this through is to use Alec Rodger's 'seven point plan'. You can use the table below to list the important tasks from the job description and then, in the columns shown, write down the personal attributes needed to ensure success in that task. In some cases there will be no entry – for example, there may be no particular physical attribute required to perform a particular desk-bound job.

Hint: you may find it easier to enlarge the table, or to use a flipchart or a whiteboard.

Tasks					
Physical Make-up					
Attainment					
General Intelligence					
Special Aptitudes					
Interests					
Disposition					
Circumstances					

You should now have a pretty good idea of the sort of person you are looking for. You can summarize the table, to make it easier to work with, and this will also give you the opportunity to spot duplicated attributes (which are therefore more important) and attributes that, while desirable, are not essential.

You should end up with a list of essential personal attributes and a list of desirable ones.

As a finish to this step, take a moment to determine which of these attributes could be acquired by training and which could not. If you are looking for someone strong, is it likely that your organization will pay to send them to the gym? If not, you are looking to recruit a strong person. However, if you are looking for someone who knows how to use a computer, you can almost certainly train a person to do this.

Finally, double-check that you have not made any unjustifiable assumptions in your analyses, such as the need for physical fitness or particular hours of work. We will be looking in more detail at legislation later but you need to be able to justify all your requirements in terms of their relevance to the job.

Congratulations. You now know what sort of person you are looking for. All you have to do now is find them.

STEP 3: CHOOSE APPROPRIATE RECRUITMENT MEDIA

What recruitment media could you use? The most usual are:

* word of mouth (such as through existing staff)
* advertising in the local press
* advertising in the national press
* advertising in the Job Centre
* advertising on radio
* using a recruitment agency (or headhunter)
* using a leaflet drop
* following up casual enquirers.

 **Activity**

At this point, you should take time out to find out what is usually done in your organization. Have a word with other managers about what they do, and what success – and nightmares – they have experienced.

As we have seen, there is legislation that governs equal opportunities (which is described more fully in the next Unit). Word-of-mouth recruitment methods may sometimes breach this. You may have a file of people who have written speculatively to you, although this type of file often includes out-of-date information and does not access the wider community where there may be someone more suitable.

Advertising and using an agency have their costs. Advertising means that you pay regardless of your success in finding someone. An agency will usually only charge you if they place someone with you – and often have offers to refund some of their fee if the person does not stay very long.

If you are putting an advertisement together, you will need to be able to design it. Also, please make sure that you are able to handle the enquiries. You would be surprised at the number of advertisers who, when asked to send the 'further information' and an application form, suddenly realize that they do not have any.

Finally, the medium you use should be the sort that this type of person will use, and that may be very different from your own preferences. You may read *The Times* and they may read the *Sun*. You may listen to local radio and they may not. If you are unsure, ask other, similar, staff what newspapers they read. Indeed, if you are replacing someone who is leaving for a similar post elsewhere, why not ask them how they found out about the vacancy they applied for? You could then consider using the same medium yourself.

VACANCY

We are a progressive, modern organization with intentions to improve even more and we now need a person to manage our recruitment process. The likely candidate will be able to show that they understand the importance of analysing requirements, producing job descriptions and agreeing person specifications. They will also need to be able to recruit new staff using the best media for the job.

The vacancy has arisen due to the imminent promotion of the current job-holder.

YOU MAY NOW CONTINUE WITH THE NEXT UNIT ON PAGE 41
OR MOVE TO THE SKILLBUILDER SECTION THAT FOLLOWS

Three Steps to Effective Recruitment

Employing new staff is a heavy investment and it is well worth taking the time to plan your recruitment campaign in some detail.

In this, as in most things, good preparation is key. Starting from the basic tasks which the job-holder is to carry out, you need to write a job description and person specification, identifying any essential and desirable attributes. Only then are you ready to decide how to attract the sort of person you require.

 Activity

Do you have a job description for your own job? If so, read it now and see how well it reflects what you do. How could you improve it?

If you don't have a job description, consider why your job exists. What are you there to achieve? What are the main tasks that contribute to that achievement?

What skills, knowledge and attitudes are critical to the successful undertaking of your job? What skills, knowledge and attitudes, while not absolutely essential, help you to do the job well?

Job analysis is a specialism in its own right so, if you found this Activity difficult, don't worry about it. By the end of this Unit you will feel much more prepared.

As with most tasks, time spent in planning how to fill your vacant position will prove well worth it in the end.

In the Fast Track section we identified three principal steps for ensuring that your recruitment efforts are well targeted and successful. We can summarize these as:

❖ Analyse your requirements.
❖ Write a job description and person specification.
❖ Choose appropriate recruitment media.

Let's look at each of these steps in turn.

STEP 1: ANALYSE YOUR REQUIREMENTS

You will already have seen the importance of job design in Unit 1. If you skipped that Unit you may like to read it quickly now, as it provides the starting point for the whole recruitment and selection process.

 Case Study

In one organization with which I worked, the IT department was experiencing significant problems with staff turnover and poor performance. When I looked at what the staff there were expected to do I realized that this might be contributing to the problems. Basically, we wanted people who were excellent programmers but who were also skilled in dealing with end-users who knew little or nothing about computers (and had very little interest in them as well) and who were good at writing user manuals to support their programs once they were complete. Unsurprisingly, we were not succeeding in getting this combination of skills within the same individual! The solution was to employ two groups of staff – those whose main interests lay in the technicalities of programming and those who, whilst understanding what could and could not be done, were not technical experts but were interested in meeting the needs of their customers and could act as 'go-betweens' between the technical experts and their users.

You may have encountered managers who have decided just to advertise a 'clerical job' and see who applies before deciding exactly what the job should entail. The idea is that the new member of staff can take on whatever tasks they are suited to, whilst the current workforce continues to do the rest. This often happens when an increase in the overall workload has led to the creation of a new post. I wouldn't normally recommend this approach as it can lead to confusion, resentment and demoralization all round. It can also be more difficult to justify your selection decisions, and we will see why this is important later in the book. So, how can you decide on your requirements?

 Star Tip

Start at the top and work down:

* Use the business objectives to determine what needs to be done in total.
* Refer to national standards for each type of job to make sure you haven't missed anything.
* Identify where teams should be used and where individuals should be the focus.
* Identify key skills and knowledge for each team.
* Make sure that team jobs fit together like a jigsaw puzzle – not overlapping but with no gaps.
* Ensure that each job is complete – this gives the job-holder a motivating, rewarding experience.

Now start at the bottom and work up:

* How does each job fit in with those with whom the job-holder will interact?
* Are lines of responsibility and authority clear and unambiguous?
* Does the sum total of all the jobs add up to an organization that will meet its objectives?

You can use national standards to help you determine what should be included in a job. These are useful not only as a checklist, to make sure you have not forgotten anything, they also help you to work out your requirements for jobs that are completely new and for which you therefore do not yet have a stock of knowledge. You can contact the Qualifications and

Curriculum Authority or your local Training and Enterprise Council to see what standards are available, although they now cover just about any job you care to imagine. (You do not have to use all the information in the standards and you do not need to think about using them for training or for qualifications, unless you think this is appropriate.)

When you are looking at the detail of a job, you can use psychometric tests to determine the attributes of the people who are successful, so that you can recruit more like them. These tests can often be administered by consultants, and there are options to use standard test 'batteries' or to design specific tests although these will tend to be more expensive. You may well have thought of other techniques such as:

Observing and talking to the person who is leaving, or to other people doing the same job, to find out exactly what it entails.

Using a job description that already exists and working from that.

Thinking about the most important elements of the work – the 'critical success factors' – and what skills are needed in order to ensure success

In the Fast Track section, we mentioned the 'critical incident interviewing' technique. Here is an example of its use in practice.

SKILLBUILDER

Case Study

In one assignment I was asked to produce a person specification for some jobs in a customer service organization. When recruiting new staff the employer had been concentrating on the technical requirements of the job specification, but she had been unhappy with the results. I asked to be allowed to interview a number of current employees, some of whom were considered to be very good at the job and others who were considered to be below average. By using critical incident interviewing I was able to identify a number of attitudinal factors that seemed to separate the good from the weak employees. In particular, the good employees regarded 'difficult' customers as needing their help, whereas the weaker employees saw them as a nuisance. This affected the way they handled them and was reflected in the number of positive and negative outcomes they achieved.

Critical incident interviewing was introduced on page 26.

The example given above is certainly not unusual. Very often we look for the technical expertise demanded by a job when, in fact, it is the 'softer' skills and attitudes that distinguish between strong and weak performers. Obviously, technical skills are often vital to a job but, where someone has the capability to develop these, I will always recruit on the basis of attitudinal factors rather than experience. After all, people can normally acquire the necessary skills but will find it much more difficult to change their basic attitude or approach.

STEP 2: WRITE A JOB DESCRIPTION AND PERSON SPECIFICATION

Now that you know precisely what your staff need to be able to do, you should write this out in a way that will be useful to you. This will normally mean producing a job description outlining the purpose of each job, the outputs required and, possibly, the principal tasks involved in achieving these outputs. You may also want to include details of any responsibility for budgetary or other resources and key contacts within and external to the organization.

One good way of tackling this task is to ask each person to write their own job description or, at least, the bones of it. Supervisors and managers can each influence the job description and perform the sorts of global checking described in Step 1 – again, by

SKILLBUILDER

> A job description describes what the job-holder has to do, who they report to, what staff they have and what other responsibilities and authority they have.

> A person specification describes the sort of person who would be suitable to take on in the job role. It may include physical attributes, knowledge, attitudes and so forth.

reference to the organization's objectives and to national standards, if appropriate. At each level, the manager should check not only that each job description is right for that job, but also that the whole set forms a coherent whole. It is at this stage that you can start to look more closely at the interpersonal aspects of jobs and include the skills and tasks needed to fit into a team, for example.

If you put the date on the job descriptions, at the time they are agreed as being correct, you will know which version you are looking at when you are reviewing it – such as when a major change occurs and at appraisal times. You can then update the job description in line with current needs. If you do this regularly, it will remain reasonably up-to-date and useful, rather than an historical record of what was required several years ago.

While there is no universally agreed content or format for a job description, here are some guidelines based on national standards for management and on common practice.

Job title: A short, descriptive name for the role.

Context: Who the job-holder reports to, and what staff they will have, plus any secondary reporting lines (known as 'dotted line' reporting, because that is often how it is shown in organizational diagrams). An extract from the organizational diagram can help.

Job summary: A relatively short description of what the job entails. It should mention all the main activities and responsibilities in general terms.

Job content: The detail of the job. All the activities and responsibilities of the job-holder – perhaps in descending order of importance. Bullet points are often better than narrative in this section.

Working conditions: This could refer to the organization's standard conditions, with exceptions written in.

Performance standards: These are the measurements that will be used to determine how well the job-holder has performed the activities listed above and how well they have carried out the responsibilities listed above.

Note: If you put something in the performance standards, it needs to relate to something in the job content. If you put something in the job content, you should consider how to measure its success and put that in the performance standards, although some activities and responsibilities may not lend themselves well to objective measurement.

The person specification is rather different, and can be quite tricky. To produce a person specification you take each task in the job description and determine the attributes required to do the work.

Your first task is to decide on the skills, knowledge and attitude needed to undertake each of the important tasks you have included in the job description. If you have conducted critical incident interviews or used a similar approach already you will be in a good position to determine these. As we saw above, it is often the attitudinal factors that determine success in a job.

See the 'Extending Your Knowledge' section for details of Alec Rodger's book.

If you find it helpful you may like to use a standard framework for guiding your deliberations at this stage. Alec Rodger's 'seven point plan' provides one such framework, which can also be used by interviewers as a model for selecting staff. This specifies the essential and desirable attributes to look for, grouped together in terms of – not surprisingly – seven major points:

1. physical make-up – for example, the ability to bend and stretch or undertake intricate physical tasks

2. attainment – for example, the level of education required

3. general intelligence

4. special aptitudes – for example, the ability to drive

5. interests – for example, willingness to work outdoors

6. disposition – for example, not easily bored

7. circumstances – for example, able to work overtime at short notice

You then need to look at all the attributes that you have identified and make a judgement as to whether each one is absolutely essential or whether it is just a 'nice to have'. You may also like to think through whether it is essential for someone to possess the required skills and knowledge on day one, or whether it is sufficient for them to have the ability to learn them in a reasonable length of time. In this way, you may turn some of your 'essentials' into 'desirables'. For example, you may want someone who can use Word for Windows but, if they can use another word processing package, they are likely to pick up the slight differences between their current package and Word very quickly. You may therefore decide that, whilst it is essential for them to have some word processing experience, it is only desirable for them to be familiar with Word. This avoids the danger of turning down an otherwise excellent candidate simply because they will take a couple of days to get up to speed.

SKILLBUILDER

You may also like to consider any aspects that affect the team as a whole, such as any gaps in preferred team roles among your current staff. If they are all wildly creative but totally impractical it may be important to find a more pragmatic, down-to-earth new recruit.

The table on page 28 of the Fast Track section can be adapted to help you put together person specifications for each of the job descriptions.

Finally, take a look at the staff you already have and compare them to their person specifications. If they do not match reasonably closely, yet they are doing the jobs well, you will need to find out where you have gone wrong. Conversely, if the people meet their specifications and are less than satisfactory, this indicates that you need to do more work. Inevitably this will happen, and simply illustrates the point made earlier about job analysis not being an easy task.

STEP 3: CHOOSE APPROPRIATE RECRUITMENT MEDIA

Now that you know precisely what you are looking for, your final task is to decide how you are likely to attract the attention and interest of suitable people.

What is likely to affect this decision?

Your choice of media through which to advertise will depend on:

❖ the likelihood of people with the required skills being available locally
❖ the way in which people in this kind of work are traditionally recruited
❖ whether you are looking for a school-leaver or someone with experience
❖ whether the post is a professional one and whether or not there are professional journals which they will read

and so on. Some managers rely on word of mouth as their principal means of obtaining new staff, inviting current employees to recommend friends or relatives whom they think might be suitable. This can be temptingly cheap and easy but there are some important drawbacks.

The main difficulties include the following:

❖ You are limiting the pool of potential employees and may not end up with the best person for the job.

❖ If you have recruited a friend or relation or a current employee into a job, it can cause embarrassment and awkwardness if the new recruit proves unsuitable.

❖ Word-of-mouth recruitment is potentially discriminatory against particular (ethnic) groups and could result in the attentions of the Commission for Racial Equality.

So what other methods of recruitment are open to you?

Some of the most widely used methods are:

❖ **Advertising**, either locally or nationally:
  • Advertising agents operate in many large cities and are able to advise on the most appropriate media for particular types of vacancy as well as undertaking the administration for you.
  • Other options include radio, posters, signs and even leaflet drops.

❖ **Using an intermediary**, such as:
  • the local Job Centre (whose services are free)
  • a recruitment agency
  • 'headhunters' who directly approach potential staff.

So, how do you choose between them? On the basis of:

❖ ease/convenience?
❖ cost?
❖ track record of success?
❖ potential for future success?
❖ what else?

You might find the following table useful. It will help you to score each recruitment medium against each measure. You can use a simple tick in the box if a medium meets the criterion in that column, or give a score out of five to reflect how well it rates in that area.

You will probably find that you need to construct a table for each type of job or each type of staff – for example, one for full-time office staff and another for seasonal packers in the factory.

	Ease	Cost	Track record	Potential
Local press				
National press				
Local radio				
Leaflet drop				
Job Centre				
Recruitment agency				
Word of mouth				
Speculative approaches				

UNIT 3   The 'Dos and Don'ts' of Selecting Staff

In this Unit, we will be covering three important areas which you need to consider when selecting the most suitable candidate to fill your vacancy. These are to:

- **act legally when making your choice**

- **select tools and techniques that are going to be of most use in determining your candidates' capabilities**

- **decide what your candidates need to know.**

Understanding these three areas will help you:

- keep within the law

- select ways of identifying whether or not each candidate possesses the skills and attributes you need

- ensure that your favoured candidate is able to make an informed decision about your job.

The 'Dos and Don'ts' of Selecting Staff

You've now reached the point where you need to select someone. Before you go down the conventional route of asking them in for an interview, spend some time considering how you will ensure that you are really selecting the person who is right for the job. We cover the whole subject of interviewing in Unit 4, and we must first put the whole process in context.

You need to gauge each candidate's match against the person specification you have prepared, so that you can choose the most suitable person.

You need to make sure that this person understands what the job is: you don't want them leaving after a couple of weeks.

You need to carry out the whole process without stepping over the line into illegal recruitment. We will take each point in turn although – as with most management functions – in practice, you will probably do these together.

STEP 1: ACT LEGALLY WHEN MAKING YOUR CHOICE

While there is more detail about legislation in the Skillbuilder section, the basic premise is that you must ensure that only truly job-dependent factors are used to discriminate between a successful candidate and an unsuccessful one.

There are many laws on the subject, with exemptions and special cases that complicate the matter considerably.

Use the following checklist to check on your job vacancy.

Can the job be done by either a man or a woman?	If not, why not?
Is the job-holder's race, religion, colour or ethnic origin relevant to the job?	If so, in what way?
Does it matter to the job whether the job-holder is married or single?	If it does, how?
Could the job be done by someone with a disability?	If so, what types? What special equipment would be required? If not, could the job be changed? If not, why not?
Should having a criminal record disqualify a candidate?	If so, what type of offences are relevant? Should you ask for a police check?

STEP 2: SELECT APPROPRIATE TOOLS AND TECHNIQUES

How will you go about measuring each candidate against the criteria you have set? One way in which you can tackle this is to write down each of the attributes you are looking for (which you should have already from your person specification) then consider the best way of assessing someone against each of those criteria. Here is an example.

Skill/attribute	Ask them	Ask someone else	Get them to demonstrate	Apply a test	Look at their work	Inspect a certificate
Can drive	✓		✓	✓		✓
Numerate	✓			✓	✓	✓
Able to supervise staff	✓	✓				
Honest	✓	✓				

In the table, we have ticked some boxes to show which methods might be used to determine a candidate's suitability against specific criteria. For example, you can tell if a person can drive by asking to see their driving licence. This will not show *how* they drive, so you could watch them drive, or even apply a short test of their ability and/or knowledge.

You could apply a test to see if someone is numerate – can they add up these numbers, or tell you what postage stamps of given denominations make up 49p? They might have passed a test and can show you their certificate. They might be able to show you an example of what they have done elsewhere.

You can ask them about supervising staff – you will know from your own experience of supervising how credible their replies are. You can also ask for a reference, and follow it up. The same applies to determine their honesty.

On the next page is a blank table which you can photocopy and use for your current selection task.

Skill/ attribute	Ask them	Ask someone else	Get them to demonstrate	Apply a test	Look at their work	Inspect a certificate

When you have completed the table, you will see what areas to cover in an interview, what questions to ask of any referees, what other tests to apply and what evidence a candidate needs to produce. This makes the job of interviewing much more straightforward and the whole selection process more reliable.

Remember that the application process can be used as a test in itself. If you need someone to use the telephone as part of their job, why not ask them to telephone for an application form or to arrange a time for their interview? As well as putting off those who do not like the telephone, it will enable you to assess their telephone voice and manner.

You can interpret the action 'asking' quite widely. Remember that you can ask for information in a CV or through an application form, as well as in person at the interview.

If you are looking for an administrator, consider how they have filled in the application form. Is it neat? Does it give you the impression that they are logically minded? If you have asked for a curriculum vitae (CV) have they tailored it specially for you or used a standard one? If you are seeking someone who will need to write letters, look at the letter which they have written to you. Are the spelling, punctuation and grammar correct?

If you decide that a test is appropriate, what sort of test will you use? Will it be a test of knowledge or skills – like an exam? Or will it be a test of their personality? The latter should really be administered and interpreted by someone who is qualified to do so, and that is outside the scope of this Workbook. However, be aware that personality tests are best when used to identify the areas to discuss in an interview, rather than being used as pass/fail tests in themselves.

STEP 3: DECIDE WHAT YOUR CANDIDATES NEED TO KNOW

Of course, your candidates will need information, too, and you must decide what to provide. Ideally, you should ask them what they want but, in practice, you need to make a judgement and collect the information before they ask.

So, what sort of information is a candidate likely to want?

The following checklist shows the types of information that you could readily offer to candidates. Against each item, place a tick in the appropriate column to indicate when to provide it. If you do not have the information, perhaps now would be a good time to collect it, before you go any further.

Remember that the selection process is two-sided, but not equal. It is therefore your job to even the balance and provide details about working conditions and so forth that the candidate may feel uncomfortable asking about.

Finally, it is a nice gesture to invite the candidate to look around the office or factory when they come for an interview. But that's the subject of the next section.

👍 **Activity**

	Before interview	At interview	With job offer
General:			
What has led to this vacancy			
What the organization does			
The size of the organization			
Other locations			
Sister companies			
Other			
Specific:			
What the job entails			
Specific responsibilities			
Level of authority			
Working conditions			
Flexible time arrangements			
Pension and other benefits			
Prospects			
Other			

YOU MAY NOW CONTINUE WITH THE NEXT UNIT ON PAGE 59 OR MOVE TO THE SKILLBUILDER SECTION THAT FOLLOWS

The 'Dos and Don'ts' of Selecting Staff

When we consider selecting a new member of staff most of us naturally think immediately about 'interviewing'. Interviewing is still a very important tool in the selection process and we will be concentrating on the skills involved in Unit 5. However, it is only one of many tools available to help select the best person for the job.

When you are considering your selection procedures, you will need to take account of the following factors:

❖ acting legally in making your choice, taking account of:
  • the Sex Discrimination Acts 1975 and 1986
  • the Race Relations Act 1976
  • the Disability Discrimination Act 1995
  • the Equal Pay Act 1970 and Equal Pay (Amendment) Regulations 1983
  • the Rehabilitation of Offenders Act 1974
  • the Criminal Justice Act 1997
  • the Asylum and Immigration Act 1996.
❖ selecting tools and techniques that are going to be of most use in determining your candidates' capabilities, including:
  • CVs, application forms and letters
  • references
  • aptitude or work sample tests and job simulations
  • interviews.
❖ determining what your candidates need to know in order to make an informed decision about whether or not to join you.

 **Activity**

Which of the selection tools and techniques mentioned above does your organization use? Does it use different tools for different jobs?

STEP 1: ACT LEGALLY WHEN MAKING YOUR CHOICE

As you can see from the previous list, there is a cluster of legislation around equal opportunities. While you do not want to turn into a lawyer, you will need to be aware of the purpose and effect of these pieces of legislation. We will therefore tackle each one of them in turn.

Sex and race discrimination

The terms of the Sex Discrimination Act and the Race Relations Act are very similar, so we will take them both together. The Acts prohibit less favourable treatment, directly or indirectly, on the grounds of:

❖ sex
❖ marital status
❖ colour
❖ race
❖ nationality
❖ ethnic or national origin.

Among other things, the provisions cover:

❖ recruitment
❖ terms and conditions
❖ access to training
❖ benefits
❖ promotion
❖ education.

 Activity

Which of the following job advertisement extracts do you think constitute discrimination under these two Acts?

Workman required

Tea lady wanted

African waiter needed for new theme restaurant

Applicants must live within 2 miles of factory

Applicants need to be physically fit

SKILLBUILDER

In the eyes of the law, discrimination can be direct – such as stating in your job advertisements that 'No women need apply' – and indirect. Indirect discrimination is where you insist on applying selection criteria with which few members of a particular sex or ethnic group can comply and that you cannot justify in relation to job need. Both types of discrimination are unlawful.

From this perspective, all the job advertisement extracts could be potentially discriminatory, although some are more obvious than others. In the case of the 'workman', the advertisement would need to make it clear that women can apply since the term, although used generically, implies a bias. To be safe, avoid the word (perhaps by using 'worker') or make it clear that both sexes are equally welcome to apply. The tea lady example is clear enough. The 'African waiter' falls under an exception and is permitted – more of which later. However, it may be that a waitress would be suitable, so this may fail on grounds of sex rather than race. There is potential for indirect discrimination if applicants within two miles of the factory are not representative of the community at large, although asking for physically fit applicants may be permitted if it is a genuine requirement, in that it allows both men and women to determine for themselves whether they are likely to be interested and eligible. Nevertheless, you need to bear in mind another Act – the Disability Discrimination Act – when determining the physical requirements for a job.

 Activity

Which of these examples represent a genuine exception to the race and sex discrimination legislation?

1. A coloured actor is required for a particular character part.

2. A single man is needed as the job entails a lot of travelling abroad and it would be unfair on a wife.

3. A woman is sought to become a masseuse in a female-only beauty salon.

4. A man is sought as a builder's labourer on grounds of required strength.

5. A local person is wanted by a company because they will get on well with local customers.

Answers:

Coloured actor: probably OK – a GOQ (discussed further below).

Single man: probably not OK on the grounds stated.

Masseuse: a GOQ.

Male labourer: no way!

Local person: borderline – best avoid.

Exceptions cover a number of different areas. For example, it is still legal to discriminate against particular groups of people where there are 'genuine occupational qualifications' (GOQs) relating to the characteristics of the job. This is where some or all of the duties require someone of a particular race or sex for reasons of authenticity (as in dramatic performances or – in the example previously given – a theme restaurant) or for reasons of decency or privacy – although you need to consider whether other members of staff can perform such work, thus eliminating the need to use a GOQ. Another exception covers the provision of special treatment for women in respect of pregnancy and childbirth.

It is legal to encourage people from particular groups to apply for vacancies in areas where they are underrepresented – 'positive *action*' – but this does extend to positive *discrimination* at the time of selection.

The Equal Opportunities Commission (EOC) Code of Practice contains guidelines on recruitment, selection and promotion and suggests that, *if possible*, someone of the same sex as the applicant be on the selection panel. There is a similar code from the Commission for Racial Equality (CRE).

The Disability Discrimination Act 1995

This Act has provisions similar to – but less stringent than – the Race Relations and Sex Discrimination Acts outlined above. You may also find that you are expected to make 'reasonable adjustments' to your place of work to accommodate the needs of a disabled applicant or member of staff.

The Equal Pay Act 1970 and Equal Pay (Amendment) Regulations 1983

You are not allowed to discriminate between men and women as regards pay and terms and conditions of employment. This provision applies to men and women employed on the same, or broadly similar, work or on work that is equal in terms of the demands of the job – but not where there are personal differences between employees (such as level of qualifications or length of service).

The Rehabilitation of Offenders Act 1974

This provides for a sliding scale of time after which convictions are held to be 'spent' and need not be disclosed to potential employers. Teaching, legal, medical, nursing and accountancy occupations are exempt. Custodial sentences of more than 30 months are never 'spent'.

The Criminal Justice Act 1997

From 1998 you will be able to ask candidates to obtain a certificate detailing any convictions not 'spent' under the Rehabilitation of Offenders Act. Under some circumstances, you will be able to ask for a certificate detailing all convictions.

The Asylum and Immigration Act 1996

Under this Act, you must ensure that anyone you employ is legally entitled to work in this country. However, because of your vulnerability to racial discrimination claims, you will need to handle this issue very sensitively indeed. Most authorities recommend that you ask all applicants the same questions or that you insist on being given an official document containing the successful applicant's National Insurance number or some other similar proof of entitlement when they start, even if National Insurance will not be payable.

 Star Tip

The Home Office *Prevention of Illegal Working: Guidance for Employers* says: 'the best way to ensure that you do not discriminate is to treat all applicants in the same way at each stage of the recruitment process.'

This is sound advice for ensuring that you comply with all aspects of equal opportunity law.

 Activity

When you are reviewing the jobs in your organization, identify any that may be exempt from the Rehabilitation of Offenders Act or the various discrimination acts. You could add these facts to the job description, for future reference.

STEP 2: SELECT APPROPRIATE TOOLS AND TECHNIQUES

The nature of our equal opportunities legislation, as well as good practice, tends to suggest that devising some sort of candidate 'score sheet' is becoming an essential part of the selection process. The sheet should clearly indicate the attributes that are crucial and then show the relative weightings of all the other attributes which you consider desirable. From this, you will be able to decide on those selection instruments or techniques that are most suited to eliciting the information you require.

On page 45 of the Fast Track section, we introduced a table to help you decide which tools and techniques you might use for each criterion of a job. We have reproduced those tools and techniques here, in a different table, to highlight the uses of each.

	Ask them	Ask someone else	Get them to demonstrate	Apply a test	Look at their work	Inspect a certificate
To get factual information	✓	✓	✓	✓	✓	✓
To predict future performance	?		✓	✓	✓	?
To exchange information	✓					
To provide subjective information	✓	✓				

The ways in which you can perform each of these techniques can be summarized as:

❖ Look at CVs, application forms and letters.
❖ Obtain references.
❖ Ask the applicant to perform a work sample test, job simulation, psychometric test or similar.
❖ Interview.

So, what are the pros and cons of each of these?

CVs, application forms and letters

These are useful for providing factual information. However, be aware that candidates' CVs could mislead – by being selective with the information provided, for instance – and may not provide the information you need.

Application forms do ensure that the information you want is covered, but they take time and effort to design and to complete and may be off-putting for busy people or for those whose written English is poor.

The signature on forms is some guarantee of accuracy.

References

These provide a useful check on the facts which the candidate has given, but the candidate is unlikely to name referees who will give a negative assessment.

You may obtain a more honest and revealing opinion if you telephone a referee rather than write to them.

You should think through what information each referee could provide before contacting them. This will ensure that you cover the points needed without wasting the referee's time.

Job simulations, work sample tests, psychometric tests or similar

If well chosen, properly administered and interpreted by qualified staff, these can predict future performance quite well by providing an opportunity for candidates to prove their capabilities or potential.

On the other hand, they can also be costly and time-consuming to administer and interpret and they are only as good as the preparation you put into deciding what you are looking for in the first place.

Interviews

Interviews can be used to exchange information between you and the candidate.

They also give an opportunity for each side to assess the other.

However, they tend to be relied on to provide predictive information that could be better supplied by other tools.

To get the best out of interviews, the interviewer (and, to some extent, the candidate) needs to be trained in interviewing techniques.

STEP 3: DECIDE WHAT YOUR CANDIDATES NEED TO KNOW

As managers, we sometimes forget that selection is a two-way process. However, because of the power differential between the two parties it can be difficult for a candidate to make sure that they have all the information they need to decide whether the job is right for them. Because of this, it is our responsibility – as managers – to ensure that we treat our candidates as 'equal partners' in the transaction by providing them with as much information about the job as is reasonable and with the opportunity to ask questions that will help them make up their mind.

 **Case Study**

I once applied for a job in the Head Office of a leading building society and was lucky enough to be selected for interview. Before the day, I was sent some background information about the job and the department and basic details about the organization's philosophy and how it views its staff.

When I arrived, the car park attendant was expecting me, as was the receptionist. Someone from Personnel welcomed me and made sure I felt at home.

The selection process consisted of an assessment centre, where all the candidates were asked to undertake a range of tasks, including presentations, problem-solving exercises and case studies. We were then shown around by a member of staff from each candidate's prospective department.

I was pleased to be asked back for a second interview. This time I was asked many more, in-depth, questions about my approach to work, how I like to be managed and how I managed my staff. I spent half an hour with someone in a similar role, who gave me the chance to discuss the real job and was able to answer some of my concerns.

By the end of the process I was in a position to decide that I did *not* want the job: my liking for independence would not have fitted with their prescriptive procedures. I was offered the job and felt able to turn it down confident that this was the right decision for both of us, rather than accepting the job, only to leave after a few unhappy months.

SKILLBUILDER

This case study illustrates a number of points. First, the recruitment and selection process plays a role in marketing an organization to the outside world. Second, the process begins even before a candidate turns up for interview, in ensuring that they know what to expect and that their arrival is expected by those who will meet them. Third, it shows how the use of a combination of selection tools can be used to get a 'rounded' picture of the candidates and test them for different skills and attributes. Finally, I suppose, it illustrates the fact that even the best selection systems can sometimes get it wrong, by offering the job to the wrong person – although, in this case, the process also ensured that the candidate was able to pick up that particular error and put it right.

All of this just goes to show that, where possible, if you can persuade Sally to withdraw her resignation, you are probably better off than trying to replace her!

 Activity

Review your sources of information. Make sure that you have a standard 'pack' that contains information about the organization, a map of where you are, details of public transport routes to you and some indication of how far you are from the railway station and so on.

Supplement this with an information sheet about each department.

Write a procedure for arranging selection interviews: include booking a room, arranging tea or coffee, notifying reception and, if applicable, security or car parking.

If it is a long time since you changed job yourself, ask a few members of staff who have joined more recently what information they would have liked to have received.

UNIT 4 Interviewing Skills

In this Unit, we will be covering the three stages of a selection interview and taking a brief look at the way in which you can use questioning to elicit the kinds of responses you require.

You will need to:

- **plan the three stages of the interview**
- **plan your questions to achieve your objectives.**

Understanding these two areas will help you improve the reliability of your interviews by:

- providing for a fair exchange of information
- ensuring that you cover everything you need to and in the depth that you require.

Interviewing Skills

Interviews are almost universally used in selection situations and, despite a number of concerns about their validity and reliability, seem set to remain as the main selection method for selectors well into the future.

However, as we saw with recruitment, the key to good interviewing is good planning. An interview progresses through three separate stages – the start, the middle and the end – each with a different aim. You will need to plan each of these in order to ensure that you achieve your objective of selecting the person best suited to do the job.

Amongst other things, this demands that you plan your questions to elicit the information you need. You will know what this is from the job description and person specification.

STEP 1: PLAN THE THREE STAGES OF THE INTERVIEW

Interviews go through a beginning, a middle and an end.

All right, you may be complaining that this states the obvious. However, as you may have found when being interviewed yourself, very many managers do not take the trouble to plan their interviews and say things at the end that, really, would have been better stated at the beginning.

 Activity

Take a few minutes to think through the potential aim of each stage, and then jot down what you would want to cover in each of them.

The start:

The middle:

The end:

I would suggest the following.

The start

The aim at the start of the interview is to set the tone and encourage a fair and frank exchange of information.

1

Make sure that your candidate is as comfortable as possible – that they know roughly what to expect and that you regard the interview as a two-way process. You can reinforce this impression by using symbols appropriately – for example, sitting at a round table and providing the same comfortable chairs for yourself and your candidate.

2

As most candidates are likely to be very nervous, and few of us are at our best when in this state, it also helps to give them some time to settle before inviting them to speak. You may therefore like to start the interview by outlining something about the job or the organization.

3

Many of us begin our interviews by asking our candidates to 'say a little about yourself'. This can actually be quite threatening. What do we mean by this? Do we want the two-minute version or the full half-hour? It's therefore better to give your candidate a clear indication as to what you expect by saying something like 'Just take a couple of minutes to give me an overview of your career so far' or 'Take ten minutes to tell me in detail about your last two jobs' – or whatever it is you want.

The middle

We are now ready to enter the next stage of the interview – the one where the main business will be done. The aim here is to cover all the aspects you need to in as effective and fair a manner as possible.

4

Now that the candidate has settled down and begun to talk more freely, it is easy for the interview to go off at a tangent. This is where your person specification comes in. If you have done your planning and listed the information you need to elicit, you should be able to guide the candidate toward telling you what you need to know, without concentrating too much on all the extraneous details. Don't worry about silences – take your time to check that you are covering everything you need to, and reassure your candidate that it is quite acceptable to think about any answers rather than blurting them out.

5

It's also good practice to make notes of each candidate's replies. This helps you remember each candidate at the end of the session and can provide evidence to support your decision in case of claims of discrimination.

The end

Once you have covered everything, your interview will be entering its closing stage. The aim here is to tie up any loose ends and leave the candidate with a positive impression of the interview. You will signal the onset of this stage by asking the candidate whether he or she has any further questions for you. Resist asking this until you are certain that you have asked everything you need to. There are few experiences worse for a candidate than to assume that the ordeal of the interview is almost over, only for the questioner to launch into a series of further questions at the end.

6

You may also need to indicate that the interview is over by giving some parting signals, such as saying 'Well, Miss Jones, I think that's all we need to cover for now ...' and then stating what the next stage of the selection process is likely to be. You might also need to stand up and show them the door.

STEP 2: PLAN YOUR QUESTIONS TO ACHIEVE YOUR OBJECTIVES

You will know what information you require by referring to the job description and person specification for the vacancy. Use the table below to list the areas you need to question the candidate about, and then write two questions for each area. The first question should be along the lines of 'Tell me about the last time you did this' and the second question should be designed to elicit some further detail.

It is best to avoid such questions as 'Why did you do that?', which can be interpreted as a challenge to their decision, rather than a question about motivation. Also, avoid leading the candidate along a path to a 'right' answer, as in 'You do have experience of this, don't you?'.

Area	General question	Detail question

YOU MAY NOW CONTINUE WITH THE NEXT UNIT ON PAGE 83 OR MOVE TO THE SKILLBUILDER SECTION THAT FOLLOWS

Interviewing Skills

In the Fast Track section we saw that:

❖ there are three stages to any interview – the start, the middle and the end – and that they need to be planned
❖ planning is also crucial in enabling you to use questions to achieve the outcomes you require.

We now look at how to improve future interviewing by delving deeper into the subject areas. First, however, you should tackle the following short activity.

 **Activity**

Think about the best interview you have ever participated in as a job candidate. (If that is too long ago to recall, try thinking about a promotion interview instead.) What made it so good?

Now think about the worst interview experience you have ever had. What made it so bad?

What lessons can you learn for your own interviewing techniques?

STEP 1: PLAN THE THREE STAGES OF THE INTERVIEW

In the Fast Track section, we revealed the astonishing fact that interviews have a start, a middle and an end. We also gave some advice on what each stage of an interview should aim for and how to go about it. In particular, we said that the aim of the first stage was to set the tone and to encourage a fair and frank exchange of information. The second stage was to cover the ground and the third stage was to tie up loose ends. There are some additional factors that will help you to plan your interviews and manage them, and these we introduce now.

There is a saying 'You never get a second chance to make a first impression'. Whilst that is true of the candidate, it is also true of you, the interviewer. Furthermore, as it is you who is controlling the start of the interview, the actions you take and what you say will set the tone for the whole interview.

In fact, your planning should start well before the interview itself. Take a look at the room you use for interviewing from the candidate's point of view. Do you have to walk through untidy offices to get there? Is the room itself dingy and unwelcoming? What can you do to improve it? Try arranging the furniture in different ways. Ask a colleague to give you their opinion. Remember that you want to put across a positive and welcoming message.

In the picture opposite, notice the comfortable chairs arranged around a small table – a low coffee table is another option. Coffee or tea for your candidate helps them to feel welcome – and may be the first drink they have had since breakfast if they have travelled some distance for the interview. A colourful picture on the wall is a nice touch – preferably a scenic view or even some modern art rather than your factory or your managing director. Blinds at the window help to avoid distractions – and are essential if the sun would otherwise shine in the candidate's eyes (or yours) or make the room uncomfortable. Finally, ensure that the room is warm, but not hot.

Consider, too, whether anyone else should be involved in the interview. Depending on circumstances, this could be someone from the Personnel department, a fellow manager, a member of staff or even a customer.

Involved	Pros	Cons
On your own	Less threatening. Can establish rapport.	You may miss important information. Personal likes/dislikes may affect outcome.
Personnel	Professional. Second opinion.	May not be very familiar with what job involves.
Colleague or manager	Second opinion.	Time. Arrangements. May view job differently.
Staff member	Has to work with new member of staff. Useful for their development.	May not be objective. Confidentiality?
Customer	Involvement. Gives interview customer focus.	Confidentiality? Time.

In Fast Track we saw that the middle stage of an interview rests on questioning (and listening). We will look at this aspect shortly.

At the close of the interview, you need to make sure that both sides have covered all they need to. You must be able to explain what will happen next, with timescales.

 **Activity**

What length of time do you need between the interview and letting a candidate know the outcome? Write down what has to be done in this period, then work out how long it will take.

Can you telephone successful candidates?

What about references? Are applications subject to these or do you request them at the short-listing stage?

If you have to wait for references or medicals, do you need to keep your second-choice candidate on hold?

STEP 2: PLAN YOUR QUESTIONS TO ACHIEVE YOUR OBJECTIVES

In the Fast Track section, we concentrated on planning a question bank derived from the job description and person specification. In this section, we take a look at the structure of the questions themselves, and the sorts of answer they may elicit. This will help you construct questions that can be used to find facts, to determine attitudes and to control the interview's progress. It will also help you avoid some of the worst interview problems.

The type of response you get to a question will depend on how the question is set, as well as its subject. Here are some question types.

Open questions allow the interviewee to respond in whatever way they choose.

Closed questions demand a short answer and do not encourage discussion.

Summarizing questions clarify what has been said. While they allow for corrections, they do not encourage discussion.

Probing questions elicit more detail about a previous response.

Multiple questions relate to two or more facts at the same time and are confusing. They should always be avoided.

Leading questions give the interviewee a clue about the answer you want. They should normally be avoided, but they can be used to encourage a shy candidate at the start of the interview.

Let's have a look at examples of these questions. The following quiz requires you to identify which category each question falls into. Simply tick the appropriate column.

👍 Activity

	O	C	S	P	M	L
How old are you?						
How much filing experience do you have?						
What was it about the job that you disliked so much?						
Do you have a driving licence?						
What sort of driving do you do the most?						
So, are you saying that you prefer to work on your own?						
Do you need to move house and would you want to take a short break between jobs?						
Would you say that you are honest and reliable?						

The first question is closed. It asks for a simple fact, whereas the question about filing experience is more open. However, this could also elicit a closed reply, such as 'Two years'.

'What was it about your job ...?' is open, as it encourages the interviewee to mention anything that comes to mind about the subject, whereas the next question requires a simple 'Yes' or 'No'.

'What sort of ...?' is a classic open question although, again, this one could elicit the closed reply 'Rallying'.

'Are you saying that ...?' could be either a leading question or a summarizing question, depending on its context. This one would probably be summarizing as it seems to be leading on from a previous response.

The next is a multiple question. How would a candidate answer if they wished to move house but not take a break? Yes or no? Although multiple questions cause few problems in a social setting, where the response can be thought through and discussed, in a stressful situation like an interview they may fluster the candidate. If that happens, you will not obtain the information you need.

Who would answer 'No' to the final question? The required response is obvious and therefore this is a leading question. The fact that it is also multiple (you could be honest but not reliable) is really not important.

So, how can we recognize these question types and create suitable questions? Here are some useful ways of recognizing and creating questions for each of the first four types – open, closed, summarizing and probing.

These might start 'Tell me about ...?', 'Describe ...', 'How did you ...?', 'What do you feel about ...?' and so on.

These might start 'Did you ...?', 'Do you ...?', 'Can you ...?' or request a specific short response – 'Yes' or 'No' – or a fact or figure.

Based on previous responses, these might start 'Am I correct in saying ...?', 'Did you say ...?' and so on. They are almost always closed questions.

Based on a previous response, these might start 'Tell me more about ...', 'What did you do next?', How did you ...?', 'What led to ...?', 'Are you saying that ...?'. They may also be either open or closed.

Now that you can recognize each question type, and you know what sort of response they encourage, how would you use them to advantage? The table below shows some ways in which each of the four main question types can be used to obtain information or control the interview.

Open questions can be used to relax the candidate and to obtain a large amount of unstructured information. Use these to find out what candidates have done in the past, about their attitudes to life and to let them show you what sort of a person they are.	**C**losed questions can be used to obtain factual data and to control the tempo of the interview. Use these to find out the essentials – for example, what notice the candidate is required to give or how many staff they have managed. Also use a closed question to bring a discussion to an end – or to silence a chatterbox candidate!
Summarizing questions can be used to check your understanding and to control the progress of the interview. Use these to make sure that you have understood the important points that a candidate has mentioned – possibly in reply to an open question. Summarizing questions also give an indication that a discussion topic – or even the whole interview – is nearing the end.	**P**robing questions can be used to follow up a thread in a discussion, following an open question response. Use these to check that the candidate really means something or that they have specific experience, and to confirm that all the details that they are giving fit together. Candidates who are generalizing about their experience or skills may not be able to back this up when probed.

A few words of caution – or wisdom – may help you use these question types well. You should use a good spread of question types in an interview. You may have seen a typical child interview on television: an experienced television reporter speaks to a child who has recently been awarded a prize for some achievement. 'Are you pleased to receive the prize?', followed by 'You must have had to work hard, mustn't you?' and so on, with the child answering 'Yes' or 'No' as appropriate. These closed questions put both interviewer and interviewee under pressure and turn the interview into a form of interrogation.

You could start the middle section of the interview with an open question about the candidate's past. Probe to obtain further details that are important to you, summarize and move on to the next topic. As a balance, use open questions at the start and closed toward the end.

Finally, you will obtain a more reliable impression of the candidate's abilities if you ask questions about how they have dealt with past experiences, rather than hypothetical ones, such as 'What would you do in these circumstances?'. Few of us really know what we would do if faced with a new, challenging, situation. Ask them to think about a real problem or issue which they have coped with and probe for information about how they tackled it and the logic or reasoning behind that approach.

Make notes of their responses and reflect some of their words back to them; this makes it apparent that you are listening and helps the interview to flow.

Fault-finder

Problem	Actions to take
Interviews very short.	Use more probing questions.
Interviews jump around.	Use their words to follow through.
You don't get the information you need.	Plan questions around the job description and person specification.
You cannot remember candidates afterwards.	Make notes of responses as you proceed. Make sure that you use plenty of eye contact.

Summary of Part I

In the four Units of this Part of the Workbook, we have looked at:

● what to do when someone leaves
● three steps to effective recruitment
● the 'dos and don'ts' of selecting staff
● interviewing skills.

We saw that you can take the opportunity to transform an often-disappointing situation – someone leaving – into a series of positive actions. By understanding the reason for someone resigning it is often possible to improve the work distribution and design and we introduced the job description and person specification as the principal means of recording the requirements for a successful recruit.

We then progressed to the different ways of finding someone suitable and ensuring that the whole process is legal and effective.

 Activity

Three actions I am going to take as a result of reading through this Part of the Workbook are:

1

2

3

SURVEY YOUR ORGANIZATION

Within this Part of the Workbook we have introduced a number of questionnaires and tables to collect information that will help you to manage staff recruitment and selection. In particular:

- job satisfaction questionnaire (page 15)
- job design questionnaire (page 18)
- Alec Rodger's seven-point plan (page 28)
- recruitment media matrix (page 40)
- selection criteria and method matrix (page 46).

Before you carry on to Part II, write a reminder in your diary to make sure that you use these. As we said previously, you could delegate tasks to a capable member of staff: perhaps ask them to review the questionnaires and tables, extend and modify them to suit your own specific needs, carry out the survey and analyse the responses.

INTERVIEWING SKILLS FAULT-FINDER

The fault-finder that we included on page 73 can also be extended. You may have found that some of the problems you encounter are not included in the four examples we gave. Use these as the starting point for a larger fault-finder and add your own observed problems to it. Discuss these problems with others in your organization, refer to the books we have listed in the final Checkpoint of the Workbook, speak to the professional institutes we also list there for their advice and add the suggested actions to your table.

When you next encounter a problem, try out the actions you have noted. You will probably find that you need to modify some in the light of experience and, eventually, you will find the fault-finder an invaluable tool. Even better, you will have incorporated the actions into your own behaviour and thus improved your interviewing skills immeasurably.

CHECK POINT

'Jack tries hard but he never seems to get the hang of it'

How to manage staff training and development

Introduction

By the end of **Part II** you will be able to:

- describe how to make the best use of your staff's skills and capabilities

- identify their training and development needs

- run effective informal training sessions

- measure the effects of training on job success.

If you are confident that you can already answer 'Yes' to most or all of the following questions you might like simply to refresh your memory by scanning the Fast Track pages in each Unit and then move on to Part III.

Self-assessment Checklist: Part II	
I am confident that I can:	**Yes ☑ No ☒**
explain the term 'self-fulfilling prophesy'	
explain how to manage people to meet different motivational needs	
outline the concept of 'team roles'	
suggest at least four different types of training need	
outline at least three ways of identifying these needs	
select cost-effective ways of meeting these needs	
find out whether the training has achieved what it was meant to	

UNIT 5 | Find Out About Your People

In this Unit, we will be preparing for the subsequent Units by discovering how to deal with people as individuals.

Understanding this will help you manage their training and development in the way best suited to their individual needs.

Find Out About Your People

Before we start on the conventional training cycle of determining training needs, providing opportunities and evaluating their effectiveness, we will take time to look at what motivates people and the ways in which they like to be treated.

Any form of development will only be effective if the individual receiving supports the reasons for it and is receptive to its method of delivery. The messages in this Unit are applicable not only to training and development but also to a wide range of management tasks, and form a good basis for managing your people in their day-to-day activities.

In this Fast Track section we will concentrate on how to deal with a person whom you currently feel needs some form of training or development. The Skillbuilder section deals with the wider issues for your organization.

 **Activity**

Choose a member of staff who has a current training or development need. Take a few moments to think about yourself and this person. Write a comparison in the space below.

In this respect	I am like this	They are like this
Example: Concentration for long periods	I can concentrate as long as necessary	Seems to get bored quickly and wander

Analyse your comparison honestly. First, look at the factors that you used in the comparison. Did they concern physical attributes – for example 'I am well dressed and he is not' – or were they about what you do – 'I arrive on time and she is late' – or about attitudes – 'I care about quality and he cares about cost'? Mark each factor to indicate 'P' for personal, 'B' for behaviour or 'A' for attitudes.

Now take another look – this time at what you wrote about yourselves. Did you concentrate on your similarities or on your differences? Mark each factor as either 'S' for same or 'D' for different.

You will probably have a mix of all markings, but you may have a predominance of some and a lack of others. This will tell you something about your own attitudes towards this person – and possibly towards others as well.

Personal attributes are the easy ones to spot, and many of them cannot be altered. The colour of one's skin, a person's height, their physical and mental make-up are not the areas for training and development.

If you concentrated on behaviours, you noticed what people do – or don't do – and how they do it. There is rarely only one correct way of doing anything, however. Did you focus on activities or outcomes? There is a world of difference between 'works hard' and 'achieves results'.

How can you know what someone else thinks? Your views about their attitudes are coloured by your interpretation of their actions – and possibly their personal attributes – in line with your own attitudes. These comments say more about you than about the other person.

Similarities and differences are on extreme ends of the same scale. There is no right or wrong here, just a matter of focus. You can use a measure of sameness to highlight areas for development between trainees and those who already do a task well. You can use measures of difference to highlight changes that need to be made in the way an individual carries out a task.

You may have found that some elements of your comparison were difficult to categorize, so here is some further help. **Behaviours** are what people do, whereas **attitudes** are what they think. Because you don't know what someone else thinks unless they tell you, you will probably make assumptions about this from what they do. Generally, **personal attributes** cannot be changed (except by cosmetic surgery). If someone is smart, they could change this, and the attribute would be better expressed as a behaviour – 'They dress smartly'. That's the test – try describing the attribute as a behaviour. If you can, it is!

The point is that behaviours can be changed through training and development, but personal attributes cannot – and are often the basis for anti-discrimination legislation. Attitudes affect the duration and effectiveness of the training and may themselves be altered as a side-effect of the development.

If you want to alter someone's attitudes it normally best to work on their behaviour first – and possibly also on the environment in which they operate. This is sometimes a 'chicken and egg' situation, however, as once their attitudes have changed, they may be more able to make behavioural changes.

So, you now know that you should concentrate on behaviour and attitudes, with behaviour being the leading indicator of attitude. We will now formalize these discoveries and add to them by concentrating on three points:

❖ Avoid stereotyping.
❖ Act as if you expect them to do well.
❖ Value strengths and manage weaknesses.

AVOID STEREOTYPING

Whilst the anti-discrimination legislation is based on outlawing some types of stereotyping, there are other types that are not covered. For example, assuming that someone is politically left-wing and liberal about the use of drugs simply because they wear sandals is a form of stereotyping. The trouble with generalizations is that they are all wrong!

We have already seen that most stereotyping is based either on personal attributes or those behaviours that are linked with personal attributes. We project on to the other person our own beliefs about the attitudes that must exist to support their behaviours. We add into the equation the interpretations of others to support our views and generally ignore those factors that tend not to fit with the overall picture.

Here are some stereotypical statements. In what ways might they be untrue? (I have made a suggestion for the first one, as an example.)

Stereotypical statement	Identified errors
Those people in the Northern sales office are all lazy.	*There may be some lazy people there – but there may be some hard workers too.*
Just like a manager – unable to make a decision.	
People over 25 years of age are over the hill and no good as programmers.	
The factory workers don't care about anything except their wage packets.	
All our customers are interested in is cost, not quality.	
Trainees just need to be told what to do; there is no need to give them exercises.	

ACT AS IF YOU EXPECT THEM TO DO WELL

We have said that the way that you interpret the behaviours of others often says more about you than about them. We can turn this around: the way you treat others will often influence how they act. So, if you think that someone is incapable of a task, and you treat them as if they are, you will probably be confirmed in your belief. If you think that they are capable, and treat them that way, you will probably find that they can do the task. We return to this 'self-fulfilling prophesy' in the Skillbuilder section.

How can you act as if you expect someone to do well?

1

By telling them how good they are, or how much faith you have in them.

2

By the way you act – allowing them to get on with the task without 'looking over their shoulder'.

3

By allowing them to take responsibility for their work – letting them decide how to do it, even if it isn't the way you would.

4

By talking positively about the outcome – 'when you have finished' rather than 'if you manage to do it'.

VALUE STRENGTHS AND MANAGE WEAKNESSES

Not one of us is brilliant at everything. We each have strengths and weaknesses. One of the lessons I learned as a new manager was that my team was as strong as the total of the strengths within it. Having everyone with the same strengths while not covering areas of weakness, resulted in a weak team. As a manager, I do not need everyone to be like me; I need people who can deal with a wide variety of situations, some of which I cannot deal with myself.

Take a moment to consider the strengths and weaknesses of your whole team, using whatever measures you consider are important. Start with yourself.

Person	Strengths	Weaknesses

What does this say about how you can use your people in such a way as to make use of their strengths? What will you do about their weaknesses? You might be able to train them, or let them work with another person who is strong in that area, or just arrange the work to avoid each person's weak areas.

YOU MAY NOW CONTINUE WITH THE NEXT UNIT ON PAGE 99
OR MOVE TO THE SKILLBUILDER SECTION THAT FOLLOWS

Find Out About Your People

We saw in the Fast Track that the one big secret to managing your staff better is to treat them as individuals. We highlighted a number of differences that could lead to them reacting to events in a very different way from the way you would react. We then gave three pieces of advice:

❖ Avoid stereotyping.
❖ Act as if you expect them to do well.
❖ Value strengths and manage weaknesses.

We will now examine each of these points in more depth.

AVOID STEREOTYPING

We have probably all heard jokes about people from particular countries, or about the differences between men and women. They are based on stereotypes. Most of us probably laugh at these jokes, because quite often they will contain a germ of truth and they ring true. What we do need to be careful about, though, is treating people as if they are typical of their stereotype. It may or may not be the case that women drivers are more considerate than men, or that male drivers are better at manoeuvring their cars than women *on the whole*. Nevertheless, within these broad groupings there will be innumerable women who behave aggressively to other road users and innumerable men who cannot park their mini in a space large enough for a bus.

When attempting to get the best out of our people, we need to remember two things. First, we should not judge people on the basis of their personal attributes, such as assuming that, because someone is nearing the age of 60, they are unable or unwilling to learn new things and, second, we should not expect other people to approach matters in precisely the same way as we do. Learning to judge by outcomes rather than processes empowers our staff while allowing us to manage the results.

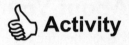

Activity

Reserve a whole day for this activity – you can fit it in with your normal work.

Pay special attention to the conversation in the office (including yours). Identify the stereotypes used and make a mental note of them.

At the end of the day, review what you have observed. How would you feel if you were a member of any of the groups stereotyped? Can you think of any people in these groups who do not match the stereotype?

ACT AS IF YOU EXPECT THEM TO DO WELL

It is probably fair to say that we all have different skills and capabilities. As a manager, it is part of your job to provide an environment in which the particular aptitudes of each member of staff can be discovered and released. How can you do this? Well, part of the secret here is to act as if you really expect them to do well.

Fact File

We tend to see what we expect to see. More importantly, our expectations can lead us to behave in certain ways that reinforce those beliefs. Research has shown that teachers gave higher marks to children who had been randomly categorized as 'above average' than to other children of the same overall range of intelligence. This could be because they marked them more generously or because their own behaviour towards those children encouraged real achievement. This is known as 'self-fulfilling prophesy'.

Similarly, it has been found that buyers who are led to expect to achieve discounts of 7 per cent generally average discounts at around that figure, whereas buyers who are led to expect discounts of 3 per cent make do with that, all other factors being equal.

It would seem that one of the secrets here is to agree stretching objectives that both of you expect can be achieved. If your staff then struggle to achieve these you need to find out why.

We are also all motivated by different things, and in different proportions. Some people have a high need for basic security, others for a sense of achievement. Some people are motivated by the thought of having responsibility for others, while others desire acceptance by their colleagues, and so on. To complicate matters even more, we are all likely to be motivated by different things on different occasions. If work is hard to come by and the bills are piling up, I am likely to take any job that comes my way, whereas if I have just won a large prize in the lottery I am more likely to be choosy about the work which I take on.

Those who are primarily motivated by the need for basic things

are likely to:

❖ want reassurance about job security
❖ avoid risks
❖ need clear instructions
❖ follow instructions but not go beyond them.

can be managed by:

❖ keeping them in the picture – especially about good news
❖ discussing potential changes well in advance and providing constant reassurance
❖ making sure that the working environment is as safe and pleasant as possible
❖ being available to 'lend an ear'.

Those who have a strong need for achievement

are likely to:

- ❖ take pride in doing a job well
- ❖ like recognition for a job well done
- ❖ set their own achievement goals
- ❖ work well without close supervision
- ❖ show initiative and commitment.

can be managed by:

- ❖ ensuring that they can see the results of their work
- ❖ ensuring that they have the resources they need
- ❖ encouraging self-development
- ❖ allowing scope for initiative and involving them in planning their work.

Those with strong acceptance (or affiliation) needs

are likely to:

- ❖ dislike upsetting people
- ❖ find it difficult to refuse extra work
- ❖ like helping others – perhaps too much
- ❖ become involved in social groups and activities.

can be managed by:

- ❖ showing that they are valued and accepted – for example, by praising them
- ❖ arranging for them to work in teams or on project groups.

Those with a need for control and power

are likely to:	can be managed by:
❖ be sensitive to internal politics	❖ giving them more responsibility over others or over resources – even if it's only the stationery cupboard
❖ seek involvement in groups with influential appeal	❖ involving them in organization-wide projects
❖ seek leadership of groups	❖ providing access to important people – even if this is only by asking them to take minutes at meetings
❖ value status symbols, such as their own office or high-performance car.	

VALUE STRENGTHS AND MANAGE WEAKNESSES

There will always be some people to whom we relate more easily than others. People differ very much in terms of the amount of external stimulation they need, their sociability, their assertiveness, their tolerance of uncertainty and their general approach to life. Some of these differences will reveal themselves in the kind of characteristics we have just looked at. Rather than see these differences as difficulties, it is more helpful to seek out the opportunities they offer.

SKILLBUILDER

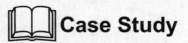 **Case Study**

Roger was finding Josie extremely hard to manage. All his other staff worked quite well together as a highly regarded team. They shared problems and pulled together to get the work done. Josie, however, seemed to be above all that. She always managed to have appointments elsewhere on team meeting days and disregarded the administrative systems designed to ensure a smooth passage of work through the department.

At first, Roger tried to bring Josie into line. However, although she always promised to behave as required – and she was consistently pleasant about it – she never quite delivered. Having failed in this approach, Roger decided to reconsider. Whilst he found it uncomfortable, the situation was not all bad. Josie was very good at building relationships with customers and suppliers. Her efforts had led to a big discount on bought-in services, plus a big new order which Josie herself was actioning. Rather than try to fight against her, Roger decided to work to her strengths. He asked the administrator to complete as much of the necessary paperwork as he could on Josie's behalf and, rather than expect her to attend team meetings, he made sure that they kept each other up-to-date on a more informal basis.

Although he would still have preferred a more team-based approach, by building on Josie's strengths Roger still managed to ensure that the department functioned effectively without requiring to bring her fully into line.

Meredith Belbin suggests that individuals have different preferred team roles and that a high-performing team will comprise people who, between them, exhibit a spread of roles. They include leaders, doers, ideas people, people who draw others in and people who criticize and evaluate. Josie is a typical 'resource investigator' – someone who excels at sourcing team needs from outside.

You may or may not agree with Roger's approach to Josie. Nevertheless, it does illustrate one way in which a manager can work with individual differences rather than fight against them.

 **Activity**

Obtain a copy of Belbin's team role inventory from your
company library, training department, local library or
bookshop. You will find the reference at the back of this
Workbook. Ask your team members to complete it and
then discuss the results with them. Even better, ask one of
your team to carry this out, and participate in it as a team
member yourself.

UNIT 6   Identifying Training and Development Needs

In this Unit, we will be covering the four types of individual training need and how to identify them. Staff experience these needs at various times in their careers:

- **when they are new to the job**
- **when the demands of the job have changed**
- **when they are struggling to meet their objectives**
- **when they have potential for promotion.**

Understanding this will help you:

- predict and plan for many training needs in advance
- motivate your staff by helping them learn the skills they need for advancing their careers
- decide whether or not training is the answer to meeting a performance gap.

Identifying Training and Development Needs

In this Fast Track section we will consider how to identify the training and development needs of a member of your staff.

This need may have arisen for any of the reasons given in the introduction to the Unit, and considering why it has arisen forms the first point. We then proceed to define that need precisely.

In the Skillbuilder section we will look at ways of considering training needs and identifying them for groups of people – possibly covering the whole organization.

STEP 1: CONSIDER WHY THE TRAINING IS NEEDED

At the start of the Unit, we gave four reasons why training might be required. Bearing the member of your staff in mind, decide now which of these reasons applies.

Unless they are new to the job, you will also need to find out what has led to the situation in which they find themselves. In what way has the job changed? What are they struggling with? What potential career move is being considered?

 **Activity**

Why is the training needed?

What is the background to this situation?

STEP 2: IDENTIFY THE NEED

There are several ways of identifying an individual's needs. They include:

- ❖ comparison against competencies
- ❖ the use of control information
- ❖ common activities
- ❖ forecasting techniques.

Comparison against competencies

Competencies are the knowledge, skills and attitudes required to do a particular job. That seems to be a reasonable place to start when determining someone's developmental needs. However, while competencies are becoming more popular, many organizations have not yet implemented them. Where can you look instead? Here are some suggestions, and you may find others of your own to add to the list.

1 Is there a job description available – whether worded as competencies or in some other way?

2 Are there national standards for the job concerned, or ones that are near enough to be useful?

3 Do you have access to a recent performance review? Does this indicate any areas of potential development?

The Skillbuilder section describes more about competencies and where they come from. If you find that you have none of the above sources, you will need to concentrate your immediate efforts on the following methods of identification and perhaps create some job descriptions and job competencies later.

Here are some examples of how you could apply the use of competencies to each of the four types of need we identified earlier.

At the start of employment

You could work through the standards that are appropriate to the job, to identify areas of strength and weakness with your new member of staff.

When job demands change

You could look at other standards to see whether these ought to be added to, or should replace, the list you have been using until now.

When someone is not performing well enough

You could jointly agree which parts of the standards they need to work on. You could do this formally at an appraisal interview (perhaps using the critical incident interviewing technique which we introduced in Part I) or less formally, perhaps by observing and noting problem areas.

To prepare someone for advancement

You could introduce them to the standards they will have to work to and identify what further skills or experience they need to succeed. Some organizations offer their staff the opportunity to participate in an 'assessment centre' where they undergo a series of tests and exercises designed to assess either their current competence or their potential in a particular skill area.

Use of control information

Control information includes such items as accident rates, complaints (and compliments!), performance against budget and so on. An increase in the accident rate may indicate a need for safety training – but do not jump to conclusions. Has anything else happened that could have caused the increase?

Analyse any control information that might be relevant to this member of staff's job performance and hence their potential training need. The following activity supplies a few initial ideas. Cross out any that do not apply and add your own.

👍 Activity

Information type	Current performance	Required performance
Accident rate		
Income targets		
Expenditure targets		
Customer feedback		
Complaints		
Rejects		

Common activities

Another way of looking at learning needs is to classify each element of a job in terms of its difficulty, its importance and its frequency. If a task is difficult, important and infrequent, it will require a higher level of training than one that is simple, unimportant and frequent. This is called the DIF rating.

 **Activity**

For each task, rate its difficulty, importance and frequency on a scale from 1 to 5. Add the figures for each task to give you an idea of the areas to concentrate on.

Task	D	I	F	Total
	1=Simple 5=Difficult	1=Mundane 5=Critical	1=Frequent 5=Infrequent	

Forecasting

The introduction of new processes, procedures, technology and so on is likely to create a number of training needs. Many of these are predictable and you should be able to build them into any plans you have for implementing the change. You may also need to deal with an employee's concerns about the reasons for the change and its effects on their job, their prospects and their security.

You can also use forecasting to assess the likely need for change by using 'leading indicators' to highlight the likely changes. Leading indicators are those events that tend to precede, and hence anticipate, something else. They could include such factors as an upturn in the economy, a more favourable exchange rate for exporters and changes in legislation. Here are two examples of how these indicators can operate.

Economic changes in the UK affect employment rates. During a boom, it becomes more difficult to find people to employ, so you may need to provide existing staff with additional training to cover the shortfall in skills capacity.

2

If changes in taxation make it more costly to move house, people may stay put and spend their money on new kitchens. If you are a manager in a kitchen unit business, you can use this to predict an upturn in business and train your staff in advance to be able to take advantage of it.

Spend some time looking at the leading indicators for your own business. Relate these to your department's situation and then to how they relate to each person's job.

You could use the exercise in a departmental meeting to form the subject of a brainstorming session, or assign the task to a member of your staff as a developmental exercise.

 **Activity**

What changes are happening now that affect this member
of staff? What timescales are involved?

What indicators might show that changes are going to (or
could possibly) occur in this person's job? How can you
monitor these indicators – or who else could monitor them
for you? What lead time is there likely to be between the
indication and the change?

Identifying Training and Development Needs

It is one thing to identify training needs for a member of your staff and quite another to look at a whole department or organization. Nevertheless, the same principles apply and this Skillbuilder section shows you how to apply the two-step approach of considering what has led to the need and then identifying the need itself to a larger group of people. It will also be of assistance when you are next faced with an individual need, as you are more likely to have in place the necessary information sources, such as job descriptions and competencies.

STEP 1: CONSIDER WHY THE TRAINING IS NEEDED

Your organization or department may exhibit training needs for the same four types of reason as an individual:

❖ because it is new to the job – for instance, it has moved into a new market or has launched a new product or service

❖ because the demands of its job have changed – perhaps because of legislation or the changing demands of its customers with regard to quality

❖ because it is struggling with the current job – as indicated by missed performance targets, for instance

❖ because it is looking to the future and wishes to acquire the skills needed to implement its strategy.

 **Case Study**

Training is not always the answer. We were approached recently to provide training to managers who need to interview staff returning to work after short periods of absence. After discussing the matter with the organization concerned, it became apparent that staff were demotivated by the production line environment and lack of control over their working day. We pointed out that no amount of interview training for managers would produce any improvement over the current situation, which would need to be tackled at a different level to encompass the whole culture of the organization, its attitudes to staff, its recruitment and selection procedures and so forth.

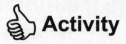 **Activity**

What is the situation within your organization or department? Which of the four reasons has led to the need for training?

What is the background to this situation?

Is training the right answer, or is some other change needed, either instead, before or in addition?

Who else is involved?

STEP 2: IDENTIFY THE NEED

In the Fast Track section, we looked at four ways of identifying an individual's needs. These identification processes can be similarly widened to an organizational level:

❖ comparison against competencies
❖ the use of control information
❖ common activities
❖ forecasting techniques.

Comparison against competencies

We introduced a definition of the difference between job

competencies and job competence in Fast Track (p. 102). This came from *Competency Based Performance Improvement: A Strategy for Organizational Change*, by David Dubois.

Competency is the underlying characteristic required to produce superior performance

Competence is the ability to meet a job's requirements by producing the required outputs

In terms of identifying training and learning needs, you may well consider that both of these are important.

The identification of job competencies is likely to result from an analysis of the job and its component tasks. You will remember that we looked at job analysis in Part I of this Workbook. Another way in which you can identify likely training needs in this situation is to use competence and standards frameworks which could be nationally or locally derived. As well as the National Standards from which National or Scottish Vocational Qualifications (N/SVQs) are derived, you might like to consider the use of the 'bodies of knowledge' provided by professional institutes, requirements from appropriate quality frameworks and codes of practice. You can then match individuals' current skills and expertise to what is required and identify any mismatches.

At the organizational level, you might wish to consider whether to base your job competencies on national standards, devise your own (which is a very large task) or create some combination of the two.

The following diagram shows the link between the aims, critical success factors, process and so on for an organization. Study it briefly and determine where competencies might be used.

SKILLBUILDER

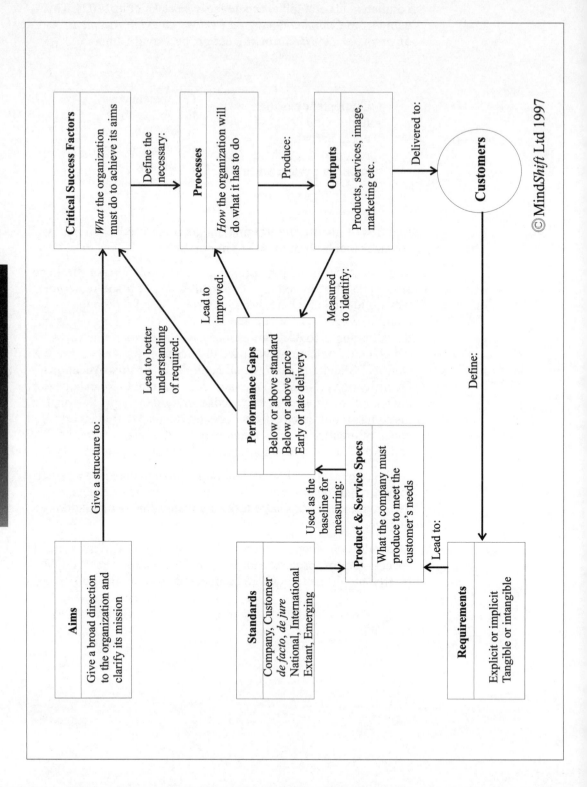

© Mind*Shift* Ltd 1997

The principal areas in which to apply competencies are those where staff need knowledge or skills to perform a task. So, while you may have spotted 'national standards' in the diagram, this really refers to the standards that apply to your outputs. The really important areas for competencies are the processes. For example, a restaurant may have aims such as 'To serve organic foods in a pleasant environment' which will lead to critical success factors that state the number of meals it must serve per week and some indication of its financial performance. These in turn will dictate a structure to how it performs, leading to processes for working the tills, cleaning the floor and buying in the coffee beans.

Measurement of performance and working out how the performance gaps are to be closed are also competencies that the business will need to define.

 **Case Study**

A large British retailer has recently introduced a competency-based selection process into its stores. The competencies required in the job are listed in a standard job template that forms the pro-forma for selection. Each candidate is assessed against each competency using a selection of the tools described in Part I and the results are recorded on the template. Obviously, even the selected candidate is likely to have some weaknesses, so the template is used as the basis for drawing up a personal development plan in their first few days at work.

Use of control information

In the diagram on the preceding page, the box relating to performance gaps introduced the idea that we can measure what we do against what we should have done – expenditure against budget, complaints against targets and so on. Just as with the Fast Track exercise where we asked you to consider one person's performance, you can do this on an organization-wide (or department-wide) basis to identify the types of gaps that exist. Are there any trends?

For example, if one person has fallen short of their sales targets, this might be an isolated incident. If many people are doing so, or if there are identifiable circumstances under which they do so, this may indicate a need for a more comprehensive training or development programme.

As mentioned before, however, these shortfalls could be caused by other factors, so you need to isolate the cause before implementing the solution.

Common activities

We mentioned the DIF rating in Fast Track. Another technique to apply is the skills matrix. As in the example below, this lists the various skills required and the people available. Each person is assessed for each of the skills. They may be fully competent, capable under supervision, or neither. (You can use whatever categories you find useful.) The final column shows an overall assessment for each skill and shows those skills for which you have sufficient cover, those that may cause problems and those that are risk areas for you. Using the matrix in this way means that you can now concentrate your training and development on the areas that currently give rise to the biggest risks.

 Activity

Create a skills matrix similar to the one below. Use it to identify your most important areas for development.

Skill	No. Req'd	John	Sue	Rav	Abi	Overall
Process new orders	4	A	B	C	C	Weak
Maintain database	2		C	B	A	OK
Answer technical enquiries	2	A	A			OK
Operate returns procedure	1		B			OK

Where:

A = Fully competent

B = Needs more experience to reach A standard

C = Needs training to reach B standard

Forecasting

Incorporating the identification of training and development needs into the organization's strategic planning gives you a better opportunity to identify the training requirements before they are needed. Rather than being caught out by a particular need – say, for training telesales operators in the details of a new product after its launch – you should be able to identify their training need, and provide for it, in good time.

Again, the skills matrix is a useful technique to use.

 **Activity**

Does your organization have a mission statement or similar? Does it have a corporate plan or a business strategy? What did it say in the latest copy of the Company Report?

What information can you extract from these documents that will give you advance notice of where the organization is heading and what development is therefore required?

Where else can you look for information? (Such as a corporate newsletter or your organization's Web site.)

Providing Informal Training Events

In this Unit, we will be covering three principal ways in which you, personally, can provide job-related training for your staff :

- **formally, on the job**

- **informally, on the job**

- **informally, off the job**

Understanding these ways of delivering training will help you:

- decide on the most appropriate type of training intervention for any particular need

- get the best out of formal and informal training opportunities as they occur.

Providing Informal Training Events

We will make an assumption that you have been presented with an opportunity to provide an informal training intervention for a member of your staff. This Fast Track section gives you guidance on how to take advantage of this opportunity and to make a success of it.

The Skillbuilder section expands on the principles involved.

STEP 1: CONSIDER WHAT TYPES OF TRAINING INTERVENTION ARE AVAILABLE

Given your current circumstances, how could you deliver the necessary training to your member of staff?

You could do so while they remain at their normal place of work (on-the-job training) or somewhere else (off-the-job training). You could prepare a training session in advance and deliver it, or send them on a training course – both of which are formal. You could coach or mentor them, interacting with them as they perform – which is informal.

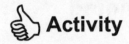 **Activity**

Consider the four types of training represented in the boxes below. In each box, write down any type of training intervention that could be applied to the situation. (An example has been shown for each, to get you started.)

	Formal	Informal
On the job	*Talk them through a process while they perform it.*	*Offer advice designed to make them think about the job.*
Off the job	*Send them on a training course.*	*Ask them to notice how other organizations do something.*

Before you decide which one(s) to use, read the remainder of the Fast Track section. The information may help you in your decision..

STEP 2: CONSIDER HOW TO DELIVER THE TRAINING

When deciding how to deliver the training, there are several factors to consider.

The type of learning required – skills or knowledge.

The availability of suitable learning opportunities within the budget and timescales available.

The disruption caused to normal work caused by someone being absent from their job or by having a learner in the job.

The individual's preferred learning style – whether they learn by doing, like to understand theories, concentrate on the practical matters or think about principles.

You may have little scope at short notice to pay much attention to the type of intervention available and may well have to accept whatever disruption is caused. However, your training provision will only be effective if you make some efforts to deal with the individual's learning style and preferences.

You may have attempted to train someone before – perhaps at work, but just as easily outside work. A relative may have said 'Show me how to...' and you did. How successful have you been? What obstacles to a successful conclusion did you encounter? The following two pages give some suggestions which should help make your training intervention successful.

1

Make sure that you put the training into context. Explain what the end goal is and how this training – or this task – fits in with that goal. When the detail has been covered, make sure that the learner understands how this has contributed towards meeting the goal.

2

Build on current understanding, leading from the known into the unknown and from the skills they have to the skills they are acquiring.

3

Train at the speed of the learner. Some people will pick things up more quickly than others, and this speed will change over the course of the training.

4

It is often necessary to allow someone to consolidate their learning before introducing more new skills or information. The point at which to do this is often quite obvious – the learner seems to regress, forgets how to do something already learned, or is simply unable to absorb any more information.

5

Provide support and encouragement. Reassure the learner that it's OK to make a mistake while learning. Point out what they are doing right, and how far they have progressed.

6

If they are acquiring a skill, they need to perform it – listening to you talk about it will not do the job. Provide plenty of practice.

7

Make the training fun – or at least enjoyable. Putting someone under pressure to learn simply does not work.

STEP 3: DEVELOP YOUR TRAINING AND COACHING SKILLS

To be fully effective as a manager, you must be able to recognize opportunities to develop your staff as they arise and to deal with them appropriately. This may mean providing a coaching session without notice for an individual or a group, to tackle an immediate need. It may mean being able to structure a more formal course of action.

You will improve your training and coaching skills by discovering what you are doing well and what you could do better and – as we said in Unit 5 – building on your strengths and managing your weaknesses. Your own manager may be able to coach you, or you may decide to attend a training course. Whatever you do, you will find that developing other people has more to do with interpersonal skills than the technical task being trained or the knowledge being imparted. Practise the following techniques.

1

Be aware of how each person responds to your intervention technique. What does this say about their learning preferences?

2

Vary your technique – tell someone how to do a task, show someone else, get another person to demonstrate – and see what differences they make.

3

Use language that is objective – 'I saw this happen' rather than 'You did it wrong'.

4

Ask the individual what they need to know and how they wish to find out.

YOU MAY NOW CONTINUE WITH THE NEXT UNIT ON PAGE 139
OR MOVE TO THE SKILLBUILDER SECTION THAT FOLLOWS

Providing Informal Training Events

In this section we will concentrate on developing your ability to recognize developmental opportunities as well as satisfy them.

STEP 1: CONSIDER WHAT TYPES OF TRAINING INTERVENTION ARE AVAILABLE

You have already seen in Fast Track that we can classify interventions as formal or informal and on-the-job or off-the-job. Formal off-the-job interventions are the subject of training courses and will not be covered in this Workbook. Similarly, as informal off-the-job interventions are more likely to be the learner's responsibility rather than yours as their manager, these are not tackled either (although you may like to consider your own informal off-the-job development).

We will therefore concentrate on the two types of on-the-job intervention – formal and informal. These may occur on a planned or an unplanned basis.

 **Activity**

Write in the boxes below as many examples as you can think of that fit the descriptions of formal and informal planned or unplanned training interventions.

	Formal	Informal
Planned		
Unplanned		

You may have thought of examples such as:

- ❖ Formal, planned:
  - special projects to develop specific skills.
- ❖ Formal, unplanned:
  - use of a computer-based training (CBT) or interactive video (IV) package to deal with an immediate situation.
- ❖ Informal, planned:
  - shadowing more experienced colleagues.
- ❖ Informal, unplanned:
  - coaching or mentoring to deal with an immediate situation.

STEP 2: CONSIDER HOW TO DELIVER THE TRAINING

The most appropriate learning opportunity to meet any particular need will depend on a number of variables, as we listed in Fast Track. These include:

- ❖ the type of learning required
- ❖ the availability of suitable learning opportunities
- ❖ the disruption caused to normal work
- ❖ the individual's preferred learning style.

Of course, these considerations are complicated by the fact that different people do not necessarily react to training events and opportunities in the same way. As you may know, open learning packs require a considerable commitment in terms of time and effort. They may not be the best learning method for people who prefer to learn in a group or for those who need the discipline of a trainer watching over them to ensure that they are doing the work. Similarly, CBT does not suit everyone. Even if your trainee is a computer genius, they might still rather interact with 'real' people than use a keyboard and mouse. Even with today's technology, many people find CBT and interactive video rather cumbersome and boring, but it can be a useful alternative to an expensive off-the-job course, or can be used to supplement other forms of learning. It may be worth looking at the training need as a whole and agreeing a variety of formal and informal interventions that, between them, best suit the situation.

These considerations will all affect your decision as to the most appropriate (cost-effective) training opportunity for your staff.

Activity

How would you classify the type of learning required for each of these tasks? Tick 'Skill', 'Knowledge' or 'Both'.

Task	🔨	💡	🔨+💡
Driving a forklift truck			
Operating a word processor			
Handling customer complaints			
Understanding how to manage a small team			
Knowing which procedure to use in each circumstance			
Sweeping the floor			

You may have started by ticking either skill or knowledge quite confidently. However, most of these tasks really require a share of both types of learning. Even sweeping the floor requires a certain amount of knowledge and, although you can learn about managing a small team simply by acquiring knowledge, it is unlikely to be of much use unless you can put it into practice – which requires a wide range of skills.

 Activity

Now consider the following learning requirements and opportunities. Match up the requirement with the most appropriate opportunity by drawing a line between them as demonstrated by the example line already drawn in.

How to use a computer software package	Book on a training course
Understanding the way something works	Demonstrate
How to fault-find on a machine	Coach, using structured questioning
How to complete a form	Provide the instruction manual

I used a naturally occurring opportunity to show you how to do the last activity – by demonstrating it. Opportunities crop up frequently if you look for them. There is rarely a single right way to provide learning opportunities, either: so you can, to a degree, capitalize on whatever opportunities occur without having to create them artificially.

 **Activity**

With so many opportunities, you may have to plan your training to minimize disruption to normal work. Consider the ideas that are shown below. Would they be suitable for your workplace? Cross out those you cannot use and add to the list further examples than you *can* use.

❖ Prepare 'mock' materials for training use, so you don't spoil the real ones.
❖ Have a training time – as many shops do.
❖ Set up a 'drop-in learning centre' near to the workplace where open learning, CBT, IV and other materials can be made freely available.
❖
❖
❖
❖
❖

 Fact File

Computer programmers keep a second copy of the application on which they are working, complete with a copy of real data, so they can test it prior to installing their modifications 'live'.

When planning the training, it is important to consider how people prefer to learn. Researchers have developed models of how people learn and Honey and Mumford, in their *Manual of Learning Styles*, identified the following four types to typify the four main learning styles.

Activists like to learn by doing something.

Theorists like to understand the theory behind things.

Pragmatists learn best when the practical application is obvious to them.

Reflectors like to think about things in order to learn them.

Other factors which affect how a learner might respond include:

Whether someone prefers to get the big picture first, or the detail – in other words, looking at the whole task or different parts in turn.

Whether someone prefers to move from the complex to the simple (as with unpeeling the components from a completed article) or from the simple to the complex (building up the article from the components).

People's speed of learning versus their consolidation of learning:

❖ Bright people tend to learn the basics of many new topics quickly but people who have a talent for the subject tend to learn more thoroughly and can eventually move on to a higher level of skill.

❖ People's learning curves may differ. If you are teaching a group, at any one time, some people may be on a 'plateau' (unable to take in anything new for a while) while others are still learning.

d

Whether someone learns best (most easily, quickly or thoroughly) when working individually or in a group:

* Those who prefer learning alone may be happy to undertake an open learning or computer-based training programme.
* Those who learn best in groups may need the motivation this affords – through companionship or through competitiveness.

Delivering the training

 Activity

Some people see on-the-job training as second best, but it can have big advantages. How many can you think of?

1.   5.

2.   6.

3.   7.

4.   8.

You may quite often decide that the most appropriate way of training a member of staff is to do the job yourself. This can be a very effective method. Most people can only concentrate on new material for relatively short periods. (You may well have found this as you have worked through this Workbook, and I find that sessions of about 40 minutes to an hour are best for me.) This gives workplace training a huge advantage over formal courses that, for logistical reasons, tend to span at least a day.

Another big advantage of training in the workplace is that you can tailor what you cover very precisely. Not only can you use real-work examples to learn from, you will also be able to find out exactly what your trainee knows and concentrate your efforts on the new elements.

On-the-job training is also a good choice for 'inducting' new employees into the workplace. The first few days in a job are daunting for many people, so a well thought-out introduction can really help them to settle in.

However, on-the-job training is not always as effective as it could be. Even short, informal sessions require clear aims, objectives and some planning if they are to be effective.

 **Activity**

Induction training plays an essential role in ensuring that your staff are effective. What should you cover in an induction training programme? How soon should each part be completed? Who should deliver the training? Complete the following table so that, next time you need to recruit someone new, you will already have the programme to hand.

What	Completed by	Who
Health and Safety rules	Day 1	Self
Tea/lunch breaks		
Toilets		
Rules on personal use of phones		
How to answer the telephone		

We have already mentioned individual differences in learning style. There are also individual blocks to learning, caused by:

❖ a negative experience in earlier life, which has led to a fear or rejection of learning
❖ a learning 'set' – not seeing the difference between one situation and another, or reverting to past behaviour patterns in times of stress (such as the familiar experience of turning on the windscreen wipers in a new car instead of the lights)
❖ a lack of interest – possibly because the material is not meaningful to them
❖ being given too much information at once – a syndrome known as 'information overload' – so that none of it is retained.

👍 Activity

Bearing in mind the above potential difficulties, suggest some ways of ensuring that your training intervention is meaningful and effective.

a

_____

b

_____

c

_____

d

_____

e

Your ideas may have included:

- ❖ breaking the subject down into manageable chunks and periodically pointing out how much progress they have made
- ❖ demonstrating how to do something
- ❖ challenging the person's negative assumptions
- ❖ giving praise and encouragement
- ❖ reassuring that it's alright to find the task difficult
- ❖ using pictures and analogies to help them find meaning in what's being said
- ❖ repeating an important exercise several times to overcome a learning set
- ❖ asking them how they would prefer to move forward
- ❖ interspersing group exercises with individual exercises so that people have a chance to 'catch up'.

You may have thought of many more, and that leads us neatly into moving forward ourselves – from what **stops** people learning to what actually **helps** them to learn. First, a short activity.

 **Activity**

Think back to a time when you learned something new. What helped you learn it? (You may find it useful to then contrast this with an occasion when you failed to learn or when you took longer than expected, and to consider what was different.)

Most psychologists would agree that the following approaches have the best chance of overcoming people's learning blocks and constraints:

❖ encouraging people to 'own' the learning by agreeing their own objectives
❖ giving them an opportunity to experience and react, rather than sit passively and just listen
❖ encouraging them to modify existing rules as a result of experience, or conceptualizing ('Oh, so this is like...') and building on what is already known (perhaps by drawing out the linkages)
❖ helping them to develop analogies or mnemonics (as, for example, ROYGBIV – the colours of the rainbow)
❖ providing examples and then asking them to put them into context themselves
❖ making sure they can put their learning into practice quickly
❖ providing them with worthwhile, sufficiently challenging, tasks
❖ ensuring that they know what's expected and encouraging them to monitor their progress against milestones (especially those they have defined for themselves).

 **Activity**

Analyse a training session that you have carried out with a member of staff recently – or one that you have been involved in as a learner. How well did it match up to the issues raised in this Unit? What would you now do differently to analyse and present the required information more effectively?

Did you:	Yes	No
identify a suitable type of intervention for the topic to be learned?		
find out the individual's preferred learning style?		
encourage the learner to be involved in setting objectives?		
structure the training to keep it short but meaningful?		
look out for signs of overload?		
help them make linkages in ways that were meaningful to them?		
give them the opportunity to try out the task quite soon after the session was over?		

STEP 3: DEVELOP YOUR TRAINING AND COACHING SKILLS

As a manager, much of the training you do will be 'coaching' – giving one-to-one assistance to fill a performance gap or develop new skills.

There is probably no hard and fast definition of the two, although training has connotations of 'showing how' whereas coaching is more to do with asking the right questions. For example, sports coaches are often less adept at their sport than the people they are coaching, but top athletes still use them and recognize their value. One of the advantages of coaching is that it helps staff develop active learning skills. By asking them to recognize what they did and what effect it had (good, bad or indifferent) you are using a much more powerful tool than simply pointing out their mistakes or praising their successes. Asking them to talk through as they perform a task is also a powerful tool for encouraging them to 'own' the learning taking place.

There are innumerable opportunities in most workplaces for managers to train and coach their staff.

 **Activity**

What coaching and training opportunities might your own workplace provide?

You may have thought of:

- ❖ when dealing with mistakes
- ❖ acknowledging achievements (which is important in that it encourages people to learn from what they have done well and provides reinforcement for that learning)
- ❖ when introducing new systems
- ❖ before and after courses
- ❖ when preparing to provide cover for staff away on holiday
- ❖ on promotion.

As a manager, you need to recognize these opportunities, plan how to exploit them and then monitor progress.

The skills required for this include:

Observing what people do and how they get things wrong. At what point do they start to go wrong? What, precisely, are they doing?

Planning sessions to maximize their effectiveness, bearing in mind the individual differences we have spoken about and the benefits of short, sharp sessions.

Analysing the reasons for problems and difficulties. Are they in a learning set? Have they failed to understand the big picture for their part of the job?

Sorting and presenting information in a logical order that suits the learner's style.

Questioning and listening to generate information and monitor progress. Adept questioning can also encourage learning in its own right.

It also helps if you are patient, good-humoured, supportive and provide constructive feedback which is accepted by the learner. So, what makes feedback constructive?

 **Activity**

Which of these 'feedback sentences' do you consider to be constructive?

'That's simply the wrong way to do it.'

'Can you tell me how you could do it differently next time?'

'I would not have done it that way.'

'I noticed that you did this...'

'That was a good method to try, even though it did not work as well as you had hoped.'

Constructive feedback should:

❖ be balanced – finding good things to say as well as bad
❖ be specific, understandable and behaviour-based
❖ be objective – 'I saw this happen...' rather than 'You were wrong'
❖ concentrate on only a few, important, points at a time
❖ allow the recipient the opportunity to identify the issues and suggest ways of improving.

Therefore, I would say that all the statements except 'That's the wrong way' and 'I would not have done it that way' are constructive – and even the latter of these could be turned into something constructive.

To summarize, there are several factors to bear in mind when planning and running a training session with your staff. These include:

Analysing the knowledge, skills and attitudes involved in performing the task successfully and deciding what exactly the learners should be able to do after the training, and agreeing these outcomes with them

Providing the sessions in short, easily assimilated chunks

Assessing the learner's prior knowledge. What do they know about the topic already? Will any similarities with other tasks help or confuse?

Consider the learners' individual styles. Should you give the context first? Should you provide a whole demonstration and then split the task into chunks – or the other way round? Should you give a demonstration and then allow the learners time to reflect or ask them to 'give it a go'?

Producing supporting materials that reflect the answers to the above

Providing opportunities for reinforcement of the training in the real work situation

Talking through progress and amending your training in the light of the comments made

UNIT 8   Evaluating the Effectiveness of Training

In this Unit, we will be covering three issues concerned with measuring the effectiveness of your training activities :

- **the one question to remember at all times**

- **the four-stage model of training evaluation and how to use it**

- **how to learn from feedback.**

Understanding these will help you:

- ensure that the training you provide is as cost-effective as possible

- ensure that your staff are able to transfer their learning into appropriate workplace situations

- learn from any mistakes and thus improve your section's overall performance.

Evaluating the Effectiveness of Training

As managers, most of us are very good at going ahead and actually getting the job done. But it is just as important to plan the task first and evaluate its success or otherwise afterwards so that we give ourselves the best chance of learning from our experiences. This means that, when considering training interventions, you need to find out whether they have achieved their purposes and, if they have not, what you can do to resolve the problem in the future.

Evaluating training is actually quite a difficult process – partly because it is easy for other events to influence the learners and obstruct the process. However, just because something is difficult doesn't mean that we shouldn't attempt it!

The first step in undertaking effective training evaluation is to remember the one crucial question – what did you want the training to achieve in the first place? It is only after clarifying this that you can begin to measure your achievement.

In order to measure their achievement, you will want to find out whether:

❖ the learners can now do what you needed them to do
❖ the training event proved cost-effective.

In this Fast Track section we concentrate on obtaining immediate feedback about how well the learners received the training. However, over a longer timescale, you will also want to know how much learning they have retained, what behavioural changes have taken place and what improvements have been made in terms of performance. You will also want to know how to obtain and be receptive to feedback and how to use it to improve future effectiveness. We take up all of these issues in the Skillbuilder section.

STEP 1: REMIND YOURSELF WHAT YOU WANTED TO ACHIEVE

Whether you are undertaking some training yourself, or setting this up for someone else, you must have some reason for doing so. Yet it is surprising how, after the event, the original reason can get lost and the training experience evaluated against different objectives.

In the Check Points at the end of this Part of the Workbook, we have included a Training Effectiveness Plan. It starts with the training objectives and includes measurable changes in behaviour and performance. Recording these expectations before you begin training will give you the necessary information against which to measure your training's effectiveness.

If you are attempting to evaluate some training for which these were not recorded, you will need to try to construct them from memory before you start your evaluation – which is a less than satisfactory position to be in.

STEP 2: ASSESS PROGRESS

 Activity

Think back to a training course that you have attended. What sort of evaluation did the trainer perform?

What sort of evaluation did you perform?

What sort of evaluation did your manager perform?

Your answers to the questions in the activity above may reveal that the trainer was interested in measuring factors such as 'method of delivery', 'pace', 'trainer style' and so forth. As an individual, you were probably more interested in whether you learned anything useful. The manager – if such evaluation took place, (which is not as likely as it should be) – was probably more interested in whether you could now do the job.

We will leave the longer-term evaluation to the Skillbuilder section and concentrate initially on immediate feedback.

Activity

How could you evaluate the effectiveness of training when someone returns from a course, or on completion of an in-house training intervention? Write one method for each of these training examples.

A one-day course on a specific computer package	
A one-week course on interpersonal skills	
A half-day in-house seminar about Health and Safety	
A one-hour coaching session for your team, on a new procedure	

The first two are traditionally evaluated by the use of 'happy sheets' – so called because (in their worst form) they often ask how happy the individual has been with the course, the catering, the booking instructions and so on and fail to measure meaningful learning. Here are some other ideas.

Ask the learner what they have learned.

Ask the learner what they will do differently now they have returned to their workplace.

Ask the learner to write a report for you (or for their colleagues) explaining the main points of the learning exercise.

Ask the learner to become trainer, so passing on their new skills and knowledge to others.

STEP 3: DO SOMETHING WITH THE RESULTS

The learners can demonstrate that the training *was* successful. What will you now do with that information? You could:

❖ use it to help decide what training others should undertake
❖ use it to inform you about the sort of training that works for this person (so you can use it again later)
❖ build on the training, so helping the individual to develop and progress
❖ plan further evaluation, to ensure that the learning is used effectively in the longer term.

The training *wasn't* very effective. What will you now do with that information? You could:

❖ determine whether the training was poor, or whether the style simply did not suit the individual or the subject-matter
❖ ensure that poor training is not repeated
❖ decide what remedial action is now needed.

Whatever the outcome, your worst option is to forget about it. That would not only fail to remedy any problems, but would also do nothing to prevent their repetition. Even more negatively, it would fail to ensure that the training received is valued by the learner.

YOU MAY NOW CONTINUE WITH THE NEXT UNIT ON PAGE 159 OR MOVE TO THE SKILLBUILDER SECTION THAT FOLLOWS

Evaluating the Effectiveness of Training

We saw in the Fast Track section that it is important to find out how successful our training interventions have been and to remedy the situation when problems arise.

We also mentioned that the first step in undertaking effective training evaluation is to remember the one crucial question:

What did you want the training to achieve in the first place?

It is only after clarifying this that you can measure your achievement.

Even informal training events incur costs – in terms of lost time and, possibly, use of equipment and consumables – so, as with any other investment, you will want to make sure that your efforts are worthwhile. Let's take a more detailed look at each of the steps covered in Fast Track.

STEP 1: REMIND YOURSELF WHAT YOU WANTED TO ACHIEVE

You may have expressed your requirements in terms of inputs – what you are putting into the training – or outputs – what you hope to get out of it. For example:

Inputs	Outputs
The training will be one-day long and cover a number of specific topics, perhaps in line with a set syllabus or to a set standard.	By the end of the course, the learner will be able to carry out specific tasks and be able to explain specified topics, perhaps in line with standards.

Inputs are very much easier to specify and measure than outputs – which is why they are used so much. However, because it is the outputs that reward your investment, make sure that your training needs are expressed in this way, and that your evaluation is based on them.

STEP 2: ASSESS PROGRESS

Various researchers have put together models of evaluation. Craig and Bittel's *Training and Development Handbook* includes an article on 'Evaluation of Training' by Kirkpatrick, who suggests that you can evaluate training in four distinct ways.

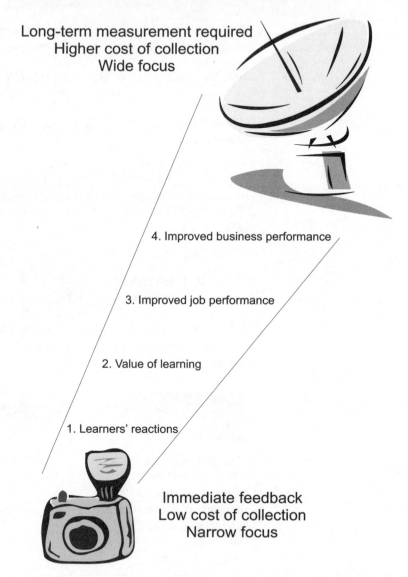

Long-term measurement required
Higher cost of collection
Wide focus

4. Improved business performance

3. Improved job performance

2. Value of learning

1. Learners' reactions

Immediate feedback
Low cost of collection
Narrow focus

We have already looked at the first stage of the model – at learners' reactions – in Fast Track. We can now progress to the other levels of evaluation, first re-posing the questions which we asked in Fast Track, but this time to get your ideas about how we might evaluate training in the other three ways that Kirkpatrick suggests.

 **Activity**

How might you evaluate the effectiveness of training at the three higher levels for the examples shown?

A one-day course on a specific computer package

Learner retention	Behavioural change	Improved performance

A one-week course on interpersonal skills

Learner retention	Behavioural change	Improved performance

A half-day in-house seminar about Health and Safety

Learner retention	Behavioural change	Improved performance

A one-hour team coaching session, on a new procedure

Learner retention	Behavioural change	Improved performance

SKILLBUILDER

There are many ways of evaluating training under each of these headings. To an extent, the answer depends on what the training was, how long ago, what the objectives were and how the learner will best respond to the evaluation. Ideally, you will want the evaluation process to strengthen the learner's motivation and feeling of success – so making an underconfident member of your team sit an exam may not be the best idea. Here are some ideas to get you started.

Learner retention

Ask your learner to:

❖ undertake a test
❖ give a demonstration
❖ present their new knowledge at a team meeting.

Behavioural change

❖ Observe your learner in the workplace.
❖ Review progress against their action plan.

Improved performance

❖ Find out whether your learner has achieved their targets
❖ Assess whether the efficiency of the section has improved.

STEP 3: DO SOMETHING WITH THE RESULTS

To make sure that any improvements are sustained in the longer term, you will probably want to review the success of the whole training programme at your learner's formal review or appraisal interview and, where suggestions for improvements are made, to make sure that these are passed on to (and preferably actioned by) the appropriate people.

Sometimes, of course, your learner's feedback will be directed towards yourself – in terms of the way you handled their on-the-job training or the support which you provided (or failed to provide) when they tried to apply their new skills in the workplace. Treat their feedback as an opportunity for your own personal development and consider all their points in terms of relevance to your own improved performance in the future.

 **Activity**

Think about the time you last sent someone on a training course. What did you do to prepare them for the course before they went? What did you do afterwards to ensure that they could apply their new skills or knowledge back at work?

What could you do in the future to help your staff get more out of the training you provide?

Summary of Part II

In the four Units in this Part of the Workbook, we have looked at:

- the one crucial rule for getting the best out of your staff
- ways of identifying training and development needs
- ways of providing training interventions
- how to evaluate training effectiveness.

We saw that someone can demonstrate one of four types of training need, making it important to be clear about what you need to achieve and what methods you can use to identify their need.

We found that, as everyone is different, we need to treat them as individuals in order to make best use of their strengths and manage their weaknesses.

We then concentrated on managing people's training and development needs and explored the ways in which you can provide the training required. These demanded that you:

- think through what is available
- consider individual differences when making your decision
- develop your own coaching and training skills.

Finally, we looked at the need to bear your objectives in mind at all times, so that you are in a position to evaluate the effectiveness of your offering. We also looked at assessing progress and what to do with the results.

Use the form on the following page to help you focus on training needs and the evaluation of effectiveness in the future.

CHECKPOINT

Training Effectiveness Plan

Name of individual: _____
Job title: _____
Name of manager: _____
Date: _____

Objective:

Timescale to meet objective:

Method of meeting objective:

Behavioural changes expected:

Target date for behavioural changes:

Performance improvements expected:

Target date for performance improvements:

How I will measure performance improvements:

Summary of evaluation plan	
At this time:	I will take this action:
While identifying needs	
The day before	
At the end of the training	
One day after	
One week after	
One month after	
Three months after	

'Managing would be easy if it were not for the people'

How to manage performance and discipline problems

Introduction

By the end of **Part III** you will be able to:

- recognize performance problems and identify their likely causes

- agree an action plan for achieving an acceptable level of performance in future

- describe how to implement disciplinary procedures effectively and fairly.

If you are confident that you can already answer 'Yes' to most or all of the following questions you might like simply to refresh your memory by scanning the Fast Track pages in each Unit and then move on to the end of the Workbook.

Self-assessment Checklist: Part III		
I am confident that I can:	**Yes ☑**	**No ☒**
explain the term 'SMART' objectives		
handle a discussion to remedy performance problems		
list three different routes to disciplinary proceedings		
outline four steps in maintaining discipline effectively		
name the five potentially fair reasons for dismissing an employee		

Problems and Solutions

In this Unit, we will be covering the three key approaches to managing performance effectively:

- **dealing with individual difficulties**
- **managing organizational issues**
- **being an effective manager.**

Understanding these approaches will help you:

- agree clear, meaningful performance objectives with your staff
- communicate your expectations effectively
- plan remedial measures
- monitor their effectiveness
- control the results.

Problems and Solutions

Performance problems can be the result of any one of the following:

❖ organizational issues, such as ineffective systems and procedures, which may require liaison and coordination at the highest level
❖ lack of effective communication and management from you
❖ lack of training or other problems to do with your staff.

The first two of these factors encompass wider issues that require a longer-term approach and, as a consequence, we discuss them in the Skillbuilder section.

The third problem area is much more immediate – and quite possibly the issue to hand at present. This Fast Track section shows you how to resolve such a situation.

DEAL WITH INDIVIDUAL DIFFICULTIES

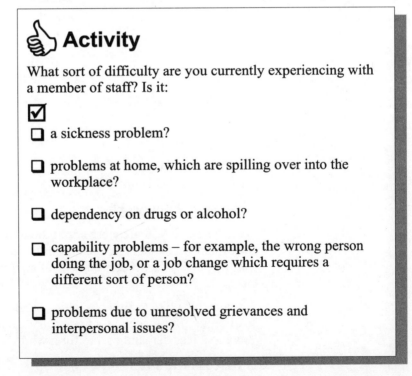

👍 **Activity**

What sort of difficulty are you currently experiencing with a member of staff? Is it:

☑

☐ a sickness problem?

☐ problems at home, which are spilling over into the workplace?

☐ dependency on drugs or alcohol?

☐ capability problems – for example, the wrong person doing the job, or a job change which requires a different sort of person?

☐ problems due to unresolved grievances and interpersonal issues?

Remember, at the moment we are talking about **performance** problems rather than **disciplinary** problems – problems concerned with lack of achievement, which may or may not be due to some fault on the part of your employee. If someone who is suffering from personal problems suddenly attacks a colleague or a customer you will need to instigate disciplinary proceedings immediately. If the problems are simply affecting their ability to reach their targets, it is more appropriate to follow a 'substandard work' or 'capability' procedure instead. Here are four steps that you can take:

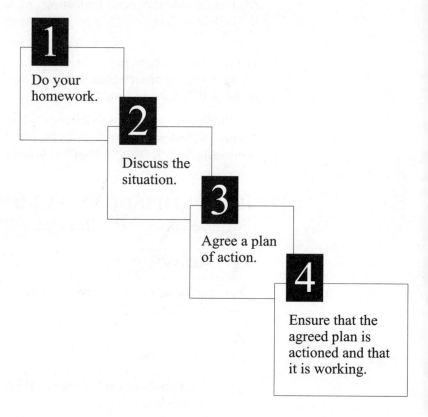

1 Do your homework.

2 Discuss the situation.

3 Agree a plan of action.

4 Ensure that the agreed plan is actioned and that it is working.

1. Do your homework

Make sure that you are clear about the minimum standard of performance you can tolerate – both in the short and longer term – and precisely how your member of staff is failing to achieve this.

You may also like to find out what concessions you are in a position to offer – such as a temporary reduction in hours or a move to a less demanding job for a while.

2. Discuss the situation

Set up a discussion with the member of staff concerned. You will need to prepare for this. What do you want to achieve from the discussion? What will be the best way of tackling it – the way most likely to achieve a positive result? The aims of any discussion of this type are likely to be to discover the nature of the problem, how long it is likely to affect them and what they are doing to alleviate it. Even if they are reluctant to give details, you still have the right to expect adequate performance while they are at work, so you need to find out how long the situation is likely to persist and whether it is likely to get worse on the meantime.

Discussions like this can be tricky. Both of you are likely to feel uneasy and it is at times like this that your interpersonal communication skills really come into their own.

 Star Tip

As well as employing your generic communication skills of questioning, listening and body language, it is helpful to demonstrate an understanding of the situation from the other person's point of view. Just like looking through a kaleidoscope, what we see is not necessarily what other people see – even with the same kaleidoscope. Each one of us has our own individual background, experience and personality and we must take care not to impose our own interpretations on other people's problems.

Before we move on to steps 3 and 4, let's take a look at how to structure such an interview. Just like the selection interview discussed in Part I, it should have three parts:

Prepare for the discussion to maximize your chances of a successful outcome and win your staff member's confidence.

❖ Set out the room in a friendly fashion by providing comfortable chairs and a clean, pleasant environment and by ensuring privacy and a lack of interruptions

❖ Note any unintended 'power' messages that you are sending by the way that your room is arranged. Do you sit on a higher chair than your visitors? Is there a large 'territorial' desk between you? Research suggests that placing chairs at approximately a 90^{0} angle can help make your visitor feel more like an equal partner in the encounter

❖ Consider the timing, including when to hold the meeting and how long to allow. Friday afternoons are the traditional time for undertaking 'difficult' discussions so that both parties have a chance to settle down again over the weekend

❖ Consider your tone – is it friendly or critical?

❖ During the discussion, reinforce these messages by:
  • offering your visitor a cup of tea or coffee
  • making sure that the sun is not in their eyes
  • taking the time to explain what they can expect from the meeting
  • explaining your exact position, particularly about the aims and objectives of the discussion
  • demonstrating your desire to listen and help, by use of your body language and active listening techniques.

Encourage them to talk.

❖ Use open questions to gain an outline understanding of the issues and follow these up with probing questions to gather more detailed information.
❖ Use reflective questions to demonstrate your understanding (for example, 'So are you saying that...?').
❖ Maintain eye contact.
❖ Suspend your judgement.
❖ Refrain from intervening with your own solutions – just listen and encourage.
❖ Allow them as much time as they need – don't be afraid of silence.
❖ If they start to become upset, encourage them to take their time. Offer them a short break if necessary – but don't let them off the hook. Some people are adept at using tears or tantrums to get their own way. Also, don't offer undue sympathy – stay objective.

Conclude the discussion with an agreement as to what has been said and any further actions to be take. Record the details in writing.

This structure of introduction–main body–conclusion is a model that you can use in most one-to-one situations. If the discussion starts to become complex, split the main body into several parts to help the discussion stay on track. For instance, where there is more than one issue involved, you could either follow each one through from start to finish or ask for a chronological account of the whole incident and analyse the interactions as they occurred.

If the situation is likely to be resolved within a reasonable time, you should offer what assistance you can to ensure that performance gets back to normal as quickly as possible. This will obviously depend on the precise circumstances.

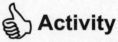 **Activity**

What options might you want to explore in each of the following circumstances?

Your member of staff is caring for a sick relative and is finding it difficult to come in to work on a regular basis.	
An unexpected bill for house repairs is causing a member of staff such concern that she is unable to concentrate on her work.	
You find that a long-standing member of staff is finding the transition from manual to computerized record-keeping extremely difficult.	

Here are some suggestions:

- ❖ If a sick child or other relative is involved, is it possible to allow the member of staff to take some hours out of their annual leave so that they can work part-time for a while? Would unpaid leave be practical? Find out how long the situation is likely to last – the solution for a one-week problem will be different from the solution to a chronic, long-term problem

- ❖ If the problem is financial, can the organization provide an advance of salary, or are there any counselling or welfare services you can refer them to? Can you offer them paid overtime? Would that help, or would it cause other problems for them?

- ❖ If the problem is due to lack of capability – where the wrong person is doing the job or a job change requires a different sort of person – is there any way in which the job could be altered to enable them to perform it adequately? Is there any further training that might help? Are there any other jobs available that might better suit them? You may not be the one to make the final decision on this but, having talked to your member of staff, you will at least be able to put your own recommendations forward to senior management, based on a detailed examination of all the possibilities.

- ❖ Explain to your staff member your requirements in terms of improved performance and discuss how these might be achieved.

 Case Study

You may remember the story of my friend Dee, related in Part I. Dee had been passed over for promotion and did not feel that she was valued by her employer.

In this case Dee resigned, but she might not have been able to do this and may well have taken out her feelings of rejection on her manager by becoming uncooperative and disruptive.

Had Dee's new manager put himself in Dee's position at an early stage, he might have expected this reaction. He would then have been in a better position to forestall it by talking things through with her, making her feel valued and important, finding out her skills and interests and putting these to good use. Working on a special project together might have been one way of overcoming any barriers that Dee put up. Alternatively, he could have coached Dee so that she would be successful in gaining a promotion later.

3. Agree a plan of action

Bearing in mind what each of you has said at the discussion, jointly agree a plan that is designed to achieve the required improvement within a reasonable time. If the performance gap is large, you will need to agree milestone steps on the way, together with timescales or deadlines, and how you will monitor these.

Depending on the specifics of the situation, their actions may include:

❖ a visit to their GP and provision of a medical report (They will need to give permission for this. If they refuse to do so, you will need to consider your response, which may be the instigation of disciplinary action.)

❖ contacting a support agency for help with dependency problems and agreeing a course of treatment which may involve time away from work, which you should normally treat as sick leave

❖ arranging for regular after-school childcare

❖ prioritizing their work in line with agreed objectives

❖ arranging a career counselling interview.

The plan could include actions on you as well as on your member of staff, such as arranging for someone else to take over parts of the job, arranging for a change of shifts or for an occupational health specialist to visit. Make sure that you follow these through as agreed. You will need to make a particular effort to follow through workplace or procedural adjustments needed by a disabled member of staff. As we saw earlier, if you fail to make 'reasonable adjustments' when required, you could find yourself falling foul of the Disability Discrimination Act.

 **Fact File**

Employers should take the provisions of the Disability Discrimination Act extremely seriously.

In a recent out-of-court settlement, a health visitor who suffered from ME won £16 000 compensation after being sacked on grounds of ill-health. She had been talking to her employer about measures that would enable her to return to work after ten months' sick leave at the time she was dismissed.

4. Ensure the agreed plan is actioned and recorded

❖ Undertake any actions as agreed and hold 'checkpoint' meetings to monitor progress.
❖ Agree what to do about any slippages.
❖ Once performance has reached the required standard, hold another discussion to congratulate your member of staff and agree any continuing actions required.

Sadly, not everyone is able, or willing, to respond to this treatment as adequately as you might wish. For one thing, someone suffering from alcohol or drugs dependency may not be willing to acknowledge their problem, or may not be ready to undergo treatment. Even if they are willing, things may not turn out as planned. If you have agreed a deadline by which the required improvement should have been made, and you still find that your member of staff is woefully below standard, there will come a time when even the most sympathetic manager may need to take a more formal disciplinary-type approach. Before your final review, make it plain that you are likely to be issuing a formal warning, and provide the employee with the opportunity to bring a friend or employee representative along. Even if, within your own organization, the proceedings that follow remain part of the 'capability procedure' rather than the disciplinary one, the activities and results will be much the same.

We are now at the stage where someone's job is on the line – whether through anyone's fault or not. If you now need to follow that route, proceed to the Fast Track section of Unit 10. Otherwise, you can continue with the following Skillbuilder to discover more about the organizational issues and how to be an effective manager.

Problems and Solutions

As already stated, performance problems can be the result of:

- ❖ organizational issues, such as ineffective systems and procedures, which may require liaison and coordination at the highest level
- ❖ lack of effective communication and management from you
- ❖ lack of training, or other problems to do with your staff.

We looked at the last factor in Fast Track. Now it is time to investigate the longer-term and wider issues that are inherent in the first two.

Before you can become aware of a performance problem you must be clear about what you expect your staff to do. The construction of SMART objectives provides one simple mechanism for ensuring that the required level of performance is understood. However, although useful, these are not sufficient in themselves to ensure effective performance. This is because, without effective communication and without the capability, motivation or necessary training, it is very unlikely that your staff will manage to achieve them.

Effective performance management also demands adequate planning, monitoring and control. As we have seen in earlier Units, everyone is different and will therefore respond in different ways to your normal management style. Some people will need a great deal of direction from you; others will prefer to go away and plan their activities for themselves. Either way, it is only fair – and good management practice – to agree with them exactly how you plan to monitor progress and what remedies are available to you in case anything goes wrong. You will also want to make sure that they have all the resources they need – including skills and aptitudes as well as physical resources such as materials and equipment – in order to succeed.

 Activity

Consider your own job for a moment. How clear are you about what is expected of you? How does your manager communicate his or her expectations? How does this suit your own preferred ways of working?

ORGANIZATIONAL ISSUES

Sometimes you may find that your staff are simply unable to achieve what you would like them to because of the way the organization is set up and run. Typical problems might include:

❖ conflicting objectives between departments
❖ communication difficulties
❖ lack of understanding of what each department is expected to achieve.

As a manager, you may be in a better position to resolve these difficulties than your staff. You may be able to raise them with your own manager, or a senior management team.

 Case Study

I used to work with the landlords of a large airport where there was a conflict between the commercial and security departments. The commercial department, whose target was to maximize profit from duty-free sales, wanted to encourage passengers to linger in the departure lounge for as long as possible, whereas the security department, who were concerned with crowd control, wanted to push them through the system as quickly as they could. The issue obviously could not be resolved 'on the ground' and the managers of each section raised the problem with the senior management team and asked for some clarification on how they should operate in the future.

BE AN EFFECTIVE MANAGER

To ensure that your staff know precisely what is expected of them, you need to:

❖ devise clear objectives
❖ communicate these effectively
❖ undertake adequate planning, monitoring and control.

Let's look at each of these in turn.

Step 1: Devise clear objectives

When you thought through your own job at the beginning of this Skillbuilder, how clear were you about what you are expected to produce in your job? Although some jobs are more easily measurable than others, it should at least be possible to clarify the main purpose of the role you are expected to fulfil. Otherwise, why were you employed in the first place?

You may have already heard of SMART objectives – it's one of those acronyms that everyone interprets slightly differently. Our preferred interpretation is:

SPECIFIC

Do they clarify precisely what they are about?

MEASURABLE

How will you know when they have been achieved?

ACHIEVABLE

Are they within the authority and control of the person responsible?

RELEVANT

Are they to do with important parts of the job – the critical success factors or key result areas?

TIMEBOUND

Have you agreed over what period they should be achieved? Are there other constraints to consider?

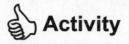 **Activity**

Take a look at the following objectives. How SMART would you say they are?

		✓			
	S	**M**	**A**	**R**	**T**
1. To have worked through this Workbook by the end of the month					
2. To have improved John's absence record before the start of the busy season					
3. To have reduced average customer waiting time from 10 to 9 minutes by the end of next year					

As far as the first objective goes, it is reasonably measurable, presumably achievable, relevant and timebound. However, you may well have thought – and I would agree – that it is not particularly specific. What is it that needs to be achieved here? If the person working through the Workbook were to clarify their purpose, it would help them to make the best use of their time and effort, to achieve their specific need.

The second objective may be relevant and it is timebound but again, not very specific. What constitutes an improvement – and over what precise period of time? However, the most problematical part of this objective is that the person who needs to achieve it is not necessarily in a position to do so. Certainly, there may be actions that John's manager could take to improve his attendance, but if John has genuine problems, these may be of little use.

The final objective is specific, measurable and timebound – and could well be achievable. To that extent, it is SMART. However, it does not sound very ambitious or inspiring and may not be as relevant as it could be. These are aspects that could be investigated further.

 **Activity**

Rewrite the three objectives in the previous activity to make them more SMART.

	✓				
	S	**M**	**A**	**R**	**T**
1.					
2.					
3.					

Our versions are:

1.

To have picked up three ways of responding to performance and discipline problems from this Workbook by the end of the month.

2.

To have interviewed John about his absence record and agreed our next steps before the start of next month.

3.

To have reduced average customer waiting time from 10 minutes to 8 minutes by the end of the season.

You will doubtless have given slightly different answers, but that is fine as long as your objectives now cover all five parts of the SMART acronym.

Step 2: Communicate these objectives effectively

The agreement of SMART objectives takes you a long way towards communicating your expectations clearly and concisely. Nevertheless, even with the best will in the world, if anything can be misinterpreted, you can be certain it will be!

Effective communication therefore begins with being clear about what you need to communicate and then ensuring that the person with whom you are talking has a similar understanding to yourself.

 Activity

How can you ensure that your member of staff has understood what you mean? Select from the examples shown.

Give reasons for your requirements

Choose your words to meet the listener's experience and capability

Encourage the listener to feed back his impression of what you have said

Ask them to explain how they will achieve the objectives

Agree how you will monitor the situation

All of these actions can be used to help ensure understanding. The principle is that you need to make your staff aware of the purpose of the exercise, so they can appreciate its context and importance and gain some form of feedback so that you can compare it with what you intended. Using the other person's style of talking or writing will help make sure that they pick up the meanings in what you say, rather than have to interpret the objectives for themselves.

Step 3: Undertake adequate planning, monitoring and control

This leads to our final step. You will recall that we have said that everyone is different and responds differently to events and activities. You need to get to know your staff so that you can make a reasonable judgement about both their capability and their preferences, in terms of your own management style.

Some people – like Josie in the example in Part II – are unlikely to respond well to close supervision. However, if your members of staff are not performing, or you do not consider they have the expertise or experience to cope, you will not be happy to give them a free rein. Perhaps you could insist on going through the planning process with them and agreeing 'checkpoints' – dates by which they must have completed small chunks of work. You could also find ways of managing which reward them with something meaningful or valuable to them for performing in the way you want, or which punish them when they don't (such as limiting their unauthorized business mileage).

You need to keep an eye on progress and communicate with them as soon as you notice that something is going wrong. You may be happy to give some staff the benefit of the doubt, while being more rigorous with others; the approach you use should depend on the staff member themselves, based on their management needs.

 Activity

During the next few weeks, undertake this exercise during your normal conversations and dealings with your staff.

For each person, find out whether they prefer close or 'arms-length' supervision and whether they are more motivated by reward or by punishment. Use this information to help you plan with them and control their performance.

Constantly update your impressions. This will help avoid problems caused by your wrong initial interpretations and will ensure that you continually modify your own behaviour to suit the changes that they will inevitably make over time.

On the next page you will see a form that you can copy and fill in if you find this helpful. There is space for you to add any further observations about how you have successfully managed each person in the past. Be aware of any confidentiality requirements if you use this.

Name	Close or 'arms-length'	Reward or punishment	Effective ways of managing

UNIT 10 — The Four Steps to Effective Discipline

In this Unit, we will be looking at the four steps you need to take when disciplinary action is required:

- **Always make sure that your own behaviour is above reproach.**

- **Give positive messages about what behaviour is acceptable and what will happen if someone breaks the rules.**

- **Don't ignore problems in the hope that they will disappear.**

- **Make sure that you follow the 'hot stove rule'.**

Understanding these will help you maintain acceptable standards of discipline in the workplace.

The Four Steps to Effective Discipline

In this Fast Track section we will offer some advice on how to deal with an immediate discipline problem, using the four-step approach. Disciplining someone is never an easy task, and the Skillbuilder section deals with ways of ensuring that discipline is maintained so that you find yourself having to deal with fewer discipline problems in the future.

 **Activity**

Before you turn the page, consider how you would want to be treated if you (albeit unwittingly) breached your organization's disciplinary rules. What would you classify as a 'positive' outcome from such a situation?

What sort of approach would be most likely to achieve this positive outcome in your situation?

STEP 1: ALWAYS MAKE SURE THAT YOUR OWN BEHAVIOUR IS ABOVE REPROACH

None of us likes to admit to being less than perfect when we have to discipline others, but you had better consider the following three factors before you commence the path to righting wrongs.

Your own behaviour should not be a barrier to disciplining your staff. You just need to be aware of how these may affect any attempts to resolve the matter.

You may have being dealing with this problems for a while now – perhaps by talking with those concerned or by taking action to avoid recurrences, such as moving staff or altering workloads. If this is the case, you will have to take a step back, to view the situation dispassionately: you may now be part of the problem.

2

You need to evaluate your own past behaviour: have you ever done something similar to the action which is causing the problem at hand? Might your staff know this?

3

Ask yourself what other, unrelated, misdemeanours you might have been guilty of.

STEP 2: GIVE POSITIVE MESSAGES ABOUT WHAT BEHAVIOUR IS ACCEPTABLE AND WHAT WILL HAPPEN IF SOMEONE BREAKS THE RULES

There are two parts to this step. The first is to ensure that the instructions you give indicate precisely the behaviour you expect, and not just a definition of unacceptable behaviour or, even worse, a vague indication of either. The second part is to let them know precisely what will happen if they persist in this type of behaviour. This may be a further warning, suspension or even dismissal. They must be in no doubt. If you don't know what the next step should be, find out before you deal with them.

I'm warning you, George. If you don't buck your ideas up, I shall have no alternative but to reconsider what my options are and think about further action.

STEP 3: DON'T IGNORE PROBLEMS IN THE HOPE THAT THEY WILL DISAPPEAR

Problems tend to get worse, rather than better, if left unresolved. This being the case, you are almost always going to find it easier to deal with a small problem in its early stages than a much larger problem later. Whatever situation you now find yourself in, now is the time to deal with it.

Even where you may consider the problem to be isolated to one individual, if others see them getting away with it, this will affect them also. They may decide to follow their example. They may decide that they cannot work in such an organization. They may cite this problem as a reason – or mitigating circumstances – for a future problem. Invariably, it is the better people who will not put up with a poor situation, and will leave – and you will be stuck with the problems.

Case Study

Within a large national organization, one of the staff was persistently late, often didn't turn up to meetings – even with clients – and took excessive sick leave (when it was known she did other work).

This situation did not suddenly happen, but gradually developed over a number of years. It become increasingly difficult to do anything about it, and managers dreaded this member of staff moving into their section.

Other staff – who knew the true situation – used her as a defence when being disciplined themselves: 'How does she get away with it when I'm not allowed to? It's unfair.'

Eventually, after an extended period of absence, she agreed to early retirement on medical grounds, which was costly for the company pension scheme and still did not address the real disciplinary issues. The organization is thus still vulnerable to repeat performances by other staff.

STEP 4: MAKE SURE THAT YOU FOLLOW THE 'HOT STOVE RULE'

Douglas MacGregor, in his book *The Human Side of Enterprise*, suggested that we follow what he called the 'hot stove rule'. Put simply, if you touch a hot stove it will burn you, regardless of who you are or what your intentions were. When you remove your hand from it, it will stop burning you. The effect is immediate and objective.

When you have to discipline someone, make sure that you do it immediately (as we have said before), that you treat everyone the same, that the disciplinary action is absolutely linked to the disciplinary problem and that you do not bear grudges. This will make the job easier for you and easier for your staff.

 **Activity**

Which of these pairs of problem and action would you say follow the 'hot stove rule'?

Mary is late for work	Her manager asks why she is late, they settle the matter and continue with their work
Chris is using the office telephone to make personal calls abroad	The manager tells all staff that they must not do this, and moves Chris to a new desk location just outside his own office
Johann is rude to a supplier	Johann's manager tells her that this is unacceptable and gives her a formal warning

The first and third examples follow the 'hot stove rule'. The action is linked directly to the problem and is appropriate.

The second example certainly does not follow the 'hot stove rule'. The manager has hidden behind a group meeting to deliver the disciplinary message (so Chris may not get the message and innocent staff may feel offended). The action of moving Chris is unrelated to the problem but acts as a constant reminder of it – possibly causing him to feel resentment at being moved long after the telephone problem has gone away.

YOU MAY NOW CONTINUE WITH THE NEXT UNIT ON PAGE 191
OR MOVE TO THE SKILLBUILDER SECTION THAT FOLLOWS

The Four Steps to Effective Discipline

As we saw in the preceding Fast Track section, there are four steps you need to take to establish and maintain effective discipline in your workplace. We will now look at how to build on these for the future.

Good managers should rarely, if ever, face disciplinary problems with their staff. After all, most people want to do a good job and are willing to be reasonably flexible and helpful. As a Personnel Manager, I used to sit on disciplinary panels and I couldn't help thinking that the manager was very often as much to blame for the situation as the people being disciplined. Had the manager been clearer about the level of conduct that they expected, been firmer, 'nipped problems in the bud' and got to know the ways in which each member of staff preferred to work, the majority of cases that I dealt with would never have come that far.

Nevertheless, occasionally you have a 'bad apple' on your staff, someone may make a serious error of judgement or a staff member loses control in such a way that you cannot ignore it. In Unit 10 we also outlined some personal problems that may manifest themselves in either poor performance or a disciplinary situation – such as problems at home, or with drug or alcohol abuse. On any of these occasions, where you suspect that a disciplinary breach may have occurred, you will need to find out the facts in order to be able to decide whether to escalate the situation or not. You may also be required to instigate disciplinary-type proceedings (whether or not they are actually known by the name) if the results of your efforts to improve on substandard performance turn out to be unsatisfactory.

Luckily, you should find that you have many of the skills you need for this already.

Let's move on to the four steps you need to take.

STEP 1: ALWAYS MAKE SURE THAT YOUR OWN BEHAVIOUR IS ABOVE REPROACH

In Fast Track we said that no one is perfect, and that you may – even unwittingly – become a part of the problem. So, how can you ensure that you remain above reproach from now on?

The first step is to define the standards of discipline that you yourself should adhere to.

SKILLBUILDER

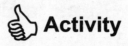

Activity

What standards should you adhere to? Look at your own job description and contract of service, plus any organizational rules or guidelines.

Be honest with yourself. Which ones can you truly say you abide by – to the letter? Which ones could you improve on? Are there any that could embarrass you?

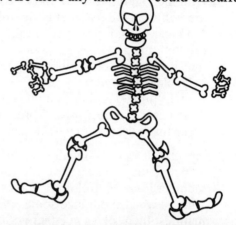

If you have managed to get through the last Activity unscathed, well done. Move on to the next step.

If not, you will have to look closely at some areas of your life. What can you do about them? Is there anything that you can now put right? Is there any behaviour that you need to stop – or to start?

If you find this difficult – and it is undoubtedly a tricky subject – take another approach. Imagine that your own manager is to discipline you on each of the matters that you identified. What would they say? What action would you be prepared to agree to?

If your actions in the past have affected your current staff – or it is likely that they may know about them, why not call a short staff meeting and make it plain that you have been reappraising what is acceptable. Tell them that you have decided that even your own actions have not been perfect and that this will now change. Ask them to do the same – and consider offering an amnesty for some types of unacceptable behaviour, on the basis that future occurrences will be dealt with in accordance with the disciplinary rules.

STEP 2: GIVE POSITIVE MESSAGES ABOUT WHAT BEHAVIOUR IS ACCEPTABLE AND WHAT WILL HAPPEN IF SOMEONE BREAKS THE RULES

 Activity

Before reading on, consider how you have given positive messages in the past – and how other people have done so.

It may be helpful to think of a specific message that you wish to convey and then consider ways of doing so that are positive.

If you carry out the staff meeting approach mentioned above, you will already have started to give positive messages. Here are some further suggestions.

1

When you set out standards of conduct, use the SMART acronym that we introduced in Unit 9.

When someone is doing well, tell them so and let other people hear you saying it.

Make sure that the incentives – formal and informal – that people receive are biased towards acceptable behaviour.

STEP 3: DON'T IGNORE PROBLEMS IN THE HOPE THAT THEY WILL DISAPPEAR

We saw from the case study in Fast Track that problems generally get worse if not dealt with. In that case, even when the persona concerned had left, the problem remained, lying dormant until the next person either did likewise or used it to support some other undesirable action.

One of the factors that sometimes prevents managers from dealing effectively with problems is that they do not know what the organizations rules are, or what the law says, or whether they will receive support from their own manager.

Now would be a good time to check on all these and clarify your own position with regard to what authority you have to discipline your staff.

STEP 4: MAKE SURE THAT YOU FOLLOW THE 'HOT STOVE RULE'

Finally, make sure that your disciplinary action will be appropriate, timely and unbiased. Once you have communicated your expectations, make sure that you respond to breaches immediately. Point out the cause and effect, explaining clearly and concisely what any further instances will lead to. Act fairly and consistently with everybody: this is no time to be subjecting yourself to accusations of favouritism or double standards, however unreasonable these may seem to you.

 **Fact File**

In a study of 300 organizations some years ago, the (then) Institute of Personnel Management found that the three most common reasons for instigating disciplinary action against a member of staff were:

- ❖ poor timekeeping
- ❖ unauthorized absence
- ❖ poor standards of work.

All these are areas in which the immediate manager is likely to need to have an input.

UNIT 11 | How to Handle a Breach

In this Unit, we will be looking at the three different routes into a disciplinary situation and how to handle each one. These are:

- continued performance problems

- long-running indiscipline

- serious misconduct.

Understanding these will help you deal with disciplinary breaches fairly and effectively.

How to Handle a Breach

There are three possible routes into a disciplinary situation:

❖ A member of staff has failed to reach or maintain the level of performance agreed under the 'substandard work' or 'capability' procedure.
❖ There is a long-running problem of absenteeism, lateness or other misconduct.
❖ A particular incident has occurred that is a serious breach of the disciplinary code.

To the extent that they are all disciplinary problems, you will need to deal with them in a similar way. However, each has unique features that could warrant a different approach. One of the keys to tackling these situations effectively is to recognize which approach to use – and then to implement it.

 Activity

In preparation for dealing with the breach you are now confronting, first identify into which category it falls:

❖ substandard performance
❖ long-running problem
❖ specific breach.

Now take a look at your organization's rules and procedures regarding this type of breach and note what course of action it expects of you.

ACT APPROPRIATELY FOR THE TYPE OF BREACH

The following Skillbuilder section advises you how to construct appropriate procedures if you do not have them already. However, in case your rules and procedures are unhelpful (or non-existent), the next few pages give some guidelines on how to handle each of these three situations.

Substandard work

All disciplinary cases are sad ones, but these are usually the saddest ones of all. Although you still need to take formal action, you are likely to take a negotiated approach. These guidelines assume that you will already have discussed the matter with the member of staff concerned and agreed joint actions, and that this approach has failed.

❖ Tell the person that you intend to instigate action under the substandard performance procedures.

❖ Arrange a meeting where the matter will be discussed.

❖ Give the person advance warning of the meeting and tell them that they can bring a friend or employee representative along for moral support.

❖ Check what authority you have for the steps you might need to take – such as a final warning or dismissal.

❖ Make sure that you know what appeal procedure exists, and let your member of staff know also.

❖ If the person does appeal, follow the appeal procedure, which will probably mean taking the case to a more senior manager for review.

Long-running issue

Depending on circumstances, you may also want to take a joint problem-solving approach to this problem, too. You should consider the cause as well as the effect. Absenteeism or lateness is often a symptom of another difficulty. If you can get to the root of this, you may be able to sort out the problem. In any case, you need to take these positive actions.

❖ Collect all the facts before you begin. Find out the normal level of lateness or absenteeism in your organization and compare it with how often the member of staff has been late or absent. Ascertain when the problem started, whether it is getting better or worse, what level you are prepared to accept, and so on.

❖ Follow the same process as for substandard performance, in terms of setting up a meeting and dealing with appeals.

Specific breach

This could cover anything from unauthorized absence to fighting or theft. It may be the result of a genuine mistake, unresolved grievance (as in Part I of this Workbook) or sheer 'bloody-mindedness'. Whatever their cause, such breaches will generally require some investigation.

- ❖ Collect all the facts before you begin, including witness statements and other evidence. Check whether the witnesses would be prepared to back up their statements in person at a hearing.
- ❖ If the situation is serious and there is a possibility of further trouble between now and the hearing, consider suspending the member of staff on full pay while you complete your investigations.
- ❖ Check the person's personnel file to see whether there are any unexpired warnings on it.
- ❖ If you consider that a criminal offence may have been committed, call in the police.

It is often good practice to escalate this type of issue to a more senior level, so that you can present the evidence to a senior manager, while allowing the member of staff to present their defence. In other respects, this hearing should be arranged in accordance with the guidelines offered for the other two categories of breach.

Finally, remember that the rest of your staff are bound to know about this incident. They will be curious about the facts of the case, how it has been handled and what the outcome is. You should be honest but discreet. Do not discuss the facts of the case with them unless there is a possibility that there might be an impact on their work.

If the person who has been disciplined is still working for you, they will need to be able to save face with their colleagues if you are to avoid further trouble. This is more easily accomplished if you follow the advice we have given about following the 'hot stove rule', being discreet about the incident and its aftermath and returning to 'business as usual' as quickly as possible.

If the person has been dismissed – or has decided to leave – you will be well advised not to gossip behind their backs. This is unprofessional and can lead to other problems with your remaining staff.

 **Fact File**

When looking at claims of unfair dismissal, Industrial Tribunals always consider whether the manager's response to the situation was within the realms of what a 'reasonable person' might expect.

 **Star Tip**

To determine what is fair and reasonable in any situation, try putting yourself in the position of your member of staff. How would you want to be treated? What other avenues would you expect to explore? How might you regard the procedure being applied to you?

How to Handle a Breach

 **Fact File**

Employment law provides for five circumstances in which you can fairly dismiss a member of staff:

- ❖ incapacity to do the job
- ❖ misconduct
- ❖ redundancy
- ❖ contravention of a legal duty or restriction
- ❖ some other substantial reason.

Even so, you still need to have fair procedures and show that you have followed them.

GET TO KNOW HOW THE LEGAL SYSTEM ACTS

What do you think is fair and reasonable? Have a look at the following cases, which were all taken to Industrial Tribunals or to appeal. Would you have said the dismissals were fair or unfair, given the five possible reasons outlined above?

In *P* v. *S and Cornwall County Council*, P intended to undergo a sex change operation. Cornwall County Council dismissed him.

S was dismissed by the Scottish National Camps Association because he was a homosexual, and parents of children in his charge were concerned about the welfare of their children.

3

Both male and female nurses working for West Birmingham Health Authority had to wear a uniform, but females also had to wear a hat. Ms B considered that the hat served no useful purpose and was discriminatory. This resulted in her being transferred into another job and suffering financial loss.

4

S had been employed by Guardian Assurance plc as an estate agent, selling insurance. He had to be registered with Lautro to get similar work elsewhere. When S left and applied for another job he was given a bad reference that prevented him from succeeding in his application.

 Activity

Delete the inappropriate results for the preceding examples:

1. The European Court of Justice decided that:
   • the dismissal was fair
   • the dismissal was unfair and covered by the Sex Discrimination Act.

2. The Industrial Tribunal decided that:
   • the dismissal was fair, due to parental concerns, not due to his homosexuality
   • the dismissal was fair, due to his homosexuality and proximity to children
   • the dismissal was unfair.

3. The Employment Appeal Tribunal decided that:
   • the requirement was fair as both sexes had to wear a uniform
   • the requirement was unfair as males did not have to wear a hat.

4. The House of Lords held that the reference:
   • was not defamatory, but negligent
   • was defamatory
   • was neither defamatory nor negligent.

SKILLBUILDER

The factual answers are that (1) was unfair as stated, (2) was fair on the first grounds stated, (3) was fair and (4) was not defamatory, but negligent. In this last case, S received £70 000 damages.

You will have gathered from these and earlier examples that misconduct can take a wide variety of forms and that what seems fair and reasonable to you may not be seen in the same light by an Industrial Tribunal or other legal power. It is therefore safer – as well as being good practice – to attempt to forestall problems and prevent indiscipline wherever you can.

It is worth looking at some of the possible causes of misconduct that you may come across. Unresolved grievances, misunderstood instructions, even retaliation against authority, may all be as much your responsibility as theirs. Listen to the messages you are receiving and be prepared to learn.

If you are prepared to dig deeper into the causes of the problem – and the causes of those causes – you may end up with an effective long-term solution rather than a quick fix to the symptoms.

Fault-finder

This cause and effect diagram shows how many factors can contribute to a single symptom. Can you use a similar technique to uncover the underlying reasons for disciplinary problems?

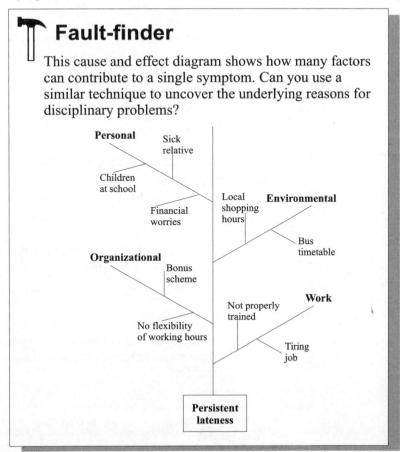

GET TO KNOW YOUR ORGANIZATION'S PROCEDURES

Tribunal cases constantly reiterate the need for managers to follow their organization's procedures. In an emergency, how confident are you that you would know just what to do? Try the following exercise and, if there are any answers you're not quite sure about, make a note to find out – soon!

 Activity

What would your own organization's procedures expect you to do in the following circumstances?

1. A woman accuses her male boss (who is your subordinate) of sexual harassment.

2. A client leaves her bag in your office while you both attend a meeting elsewhere, and returns to find that is has disappeared.

3. You arrive in your workplace to find two of your subordinates having a stand-up fight, with colleagues egging them on.

4. You see in the local newspaper that your personal assistant has been fined £150 for shoplifting.

5. A senior manager complains to you that a member of your staff slammed down the telephone on him earlier in the day.

CHECKLIST FOR A DISCIPLINARY PROCEDURE

If you need to construct a disciplinary procedure – or you want to check that the one you have is up to standard – use this checklist to make sure that you have included everything. It supports the guidance offered by ACAS.

Disciplinary Procedure Checklist

Your procedure should:

✓ ✗

- ❖ be in writing ☐
- ❖ state to whom it applies and be made available to them ☐
- ❖ be uncomplicated and timely to administer ☐
- ❖ show what sort of action may be taken ☐
- ❖ specify who has the authority to carry out the procedures ☐
- ❖ specify how staff will be informed of complaints and what they can do about these ☐
- ❖ offer the member of staff the right to bring a colleague or friend to a formal hearing for moral support ☐
- ❖ provide for dismissal for gross misconduct and persistent offenders only ☐
- ❖ require that investigations are made before a case is heard, and that a case is heard before a decision is made ☐
- ❖ ensure that the outcome of the process is communicated to the employee, with an explanation ☐
- ❖ include an appeal process ☐

You should also ensure that the procedure does not discriminate on racial or sexual grounds (along the same lines as the equal opportunities legislation), on grounds of length of service or on the basis of trade union membership.

SKILLBUILDER

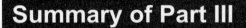

Summary of Part III

In the three Units of this Part of the Workbook, we have looked at:

- how to manage performance problems
- the four steps to effective discipline
- what to do when someone breaches your disciplinary rules.

We saw that there can be problems at organizational and individual levels. In particular, we saw that the formulation of SMART objectives can help clarify your requirements in your own mind and provide a goal for your members of staff to work towards. We also saw how you can agree monitoring and control techniques to ensure that you catch problems before they become too severe or entrenched.

We then explored the four steps to effective discipline and finally how to deal with breaches.

 Activity

Three actions I am going to take as a result of reading through this Part of the Workbook are:

1

2

3

Maintaining Your Skills

Now that you have completed Parts I to III of this Workbook, it would be a good time to review your objectives and determine whether you have met them. How confident are you that you can now answer all the points at the beginning of each Part? (Try them now.) Are you in a better position to handle the problems your staff are likely to throw at you?

If you have completed all the activities as you have read through, you should be able to answer 'Yes' to most, or all, of these questions. Nevertheless, we have covered some very tricky material in this Workbook and it would be surprising if you felt fully confident about all of it. Therefore, you might like to try the final Activities on the next page. If you are studying for a qualification – such as an NVQ in Management – you will find that these Activities will provide evidence of your understanding in this area of management.

Thank you for reading *Managing People*. We hope that you have enjoyed the experience and found it useful.

Good luck!

Activity 1

Have a look at a selection of vacancies for the type of work with which you are familiar. Critically evaluate them. If you were looking for another job, would you be attracted to the posts as advertised? Why? What do your colleagues think?

Make a list of good and bad practice in recruitment advertising, based on your results. What can you do to ensure that your recruitment advertisements reflect best practice?

 # Activity 2

If you have a training section in your organization, make an appointment to visit the manager there. Discuss the points made in this Workbook and obtain their views. How can the training manager help you in determining and meeting your staff's training needs?

If you do not have a manager responsible for training, talk to colleagues from other departments. How do they go about identifying training needs? What training solutions have they used in the past, and how successful were they? Is there anything you can do on a collaborative basis to help your staff work better together?

 # Activity 3

We have concentrated on performance problems in this Workbook, but they are not the only problems you may face as a manager. As we saw in Part I, unresolved grievances can be instrumental in resignations or can cause motivational or disciplinary problems.

Obtain a copy of your organization's grievance procedure, and any other procedures covering such instances as bullying or harassment at work. Using these procedures and the points in the Workbook, make a note of how you would tackle problems of this kind. What would you do differently, and what would you do the same, in each situation?

Extending Your Knowledge

This Workbook necessarily provides only a brief overview of some important and complex topics. If it has whetted your appetite for more, here are some further books and useful addresses to keep you on the knowledge trail.

m c ī

Management Charter Initiative
10-12 Russell Square, London, WC1B 5BZ

the Institute of Management
Cottingham Road, Corby NN17 1TT

Further Avenues to Explore

The Seven Point Plan
Rodger, A., 1952. London: NIIP.

The One Minute Manager
Blanchard, K., 1983.
London: Fontana.

Manual of Learning Styles, 3rd ed.
Honey, P. and Mumford, A., 1992.
Maidenhead: Peter Honey Publications.

The Human Side of Enterprise
McGregor, D., 1970.
Maidenhead: McGraw Hill.

Problem People ... and How to Manage Them
Peter Honey, 1992.
London: IPM Books.

Institute of Personnel and Development
Camp Road, London
SW19 4UX

Organizations

A Manager's Guide to Self Development, 3rd ed.
Mike Pedler, John Burgoyne, Tom Boydell, 1984.
London: McGraw Hill.

The Learning Company: A Strategy for Sustainable Development
Mike Pedler, John Burgoyne, Tom Boydell, 1991.
London: McGraw Hill.

Evaluating Training Programmes: The Four Levels
Kirkpatrick, D.L., 1994. San Francisco: McGraw Hill.

Team Roles at Work
Belbin, M., 1993.
Oxford: Butterworth Heinemann.

Building a Better Team
Peter Moxon, 1993.
Aldershot: Gower.

Interesting Books

Competency Based Performance Improvement: A Strategy for Organizational Change
Dubois, D., 1993.
USA: Human Resource Development

CHECKPOINT